D0515567

A JOURNEY FOR ALL SEASONS

A Journey for All Seasons

A CROSS-COUNTRY CELEBRATION OF THE NATURAL WORLD

JOHN A. KINCH AND CONTRIBUTING WRITERS

ILLUSTRATIONS BY ANDREW C. MOTT

A NATURE CONSERVANCY BOOK

The Lyons Press

Copyright © 2000 by The Nature Conservancy

Illustrations copyright © 2000 by Andrew C. Mott

All Rights Reserved. No part of this book may be reproduced in any manner without the express written consent of the publisher, except in the case of brief excerpts in critical reviews and articles. All inquiries should be addressed to: The Lyons Press, 123 West 18 Street, New York, New York 10011.

FIRST EDITION

Printed in the United States of America
Design and composition by Cindy LaBreacht

Jacket photographs (front):
Upper left: Pine Butte Preserve, Montana © Harold E. Malde
Lower left: Silver Creek Preserve, Idaho © Guy Bonnivier / The Nature Conservancy
Upper right: San Miguel River Preserve, Colorado © Harold E. Malde
Lower right: Comertown Pothole Prairie Reserve, Montana © Harold E. Malde
Back cover photograph © Janet Haas / The Nature Conservancy

10 9 8 7 6 5 4 3 2 1

Library of Congress Cataloging-in-Publication Data

Kinch, John A.
    A journey for all seasons : a cross country celebration of the natural world /
John A. Kinch. — 1st ed.
        p.   cm.
    "A Nature Conservancy book."
    ISBN 1-55821-943-9
    1. Natural history—United States.   2. Seasons—United States.
3. Natural areas—United States.   I. Title.
QH104.K54   1999
508.73—dc21   99-40930
                                                                    CIP

THE NATURE CONSERVANCY

The mission of The Nature Conservancy is to preserve plants, animals, and natural communities that represent the diversity of life on Earth by protecting the lands and waters they need to survive.

The Conservancy operates the largest private system of nature sanctuaries in the world—1,340 preserves in the United States alone. All of them safeguard imperiled species of plants and animals. The Conservancy also works internationally, helping like-minded partners protect land in Latin America, the Caribbean, Asia, and the Pacific.

Come visit.

Walk quietly.

Listen carefully.

You'll see and marvel at the astounding diversity of life.

Contents

WINTER
128

ACKNOWLEDGMENTS

CONTRIBUTING WRITERS:

Joseph Barbato
Tracey Bedford
Cara Byington
Beth Duris
Patty Housman

We would like to thank the following people who contributed pieces to this book about the places where they work: Erin Dovichin, Alaska; Melinda Helmick, Colorado; Melinda Rennert, Hawai`i; Janet Kampf, Minnesota; John Sommerhof, Iowa and Missouri; Amy Parish, Mississippi; Joseph Short, Nebraska; Kathleen Conrad, New York; Ida Lynch, North Carolina; Stephen Anderson, Oregon; Lori Klein, Pennsylvania; Scott Comings, Rhode Island; Andrea McQuay, Tennessee; Libby Ellis, Utah; Rob Riordan, Virginia; Leslie Alysworth, Texas and West Virginia.

We would also like to thank the many Nature Conservancy staffers, interns, volunteers, and partners who contributed to the development of this book, especially: Katie Hayes, Shaun Flynn, Ed Wilk, Mary McIntyre, Jeffrey Cooper, Lance Peacock, Mark Silverstein, Stephen Patton, Lise Hanners, Donna Schneider, Nancy Braker, Carol Largey, Mark Chiappone, Cathy Yi, Meg Jones, Chris O'Brien, Trish Klahr, Stan Gray, Rick Blom, Max D. Hutchinson, Raymond Smith, Jeffrey Maddox, Chip Sutton, Ruth Palmer, Richard Martin, Barbara Vickery, Doug Samson, Dave Ewert, Julie Muchlberg, David Hanna, Roy Burlington, Caryl Alarcon, Gian Galassi, Peter Benson, Karen Ruhren, Patrick McCarthy, Brian Richter, Michael Scheibel, Charlie Quinn, Pam Robinson, Jean Harrigal, Gabby Call, Sally Rollins, Tom Ledbetter, Maryke Gillis, Pam McAllister, Becky Abel, Cate Harrington, Phil Shepard, Lynda Richardson.

The idea to compile these natural events into a book grew from The Nature Conservancy's *Natural Events Almanac*, an annual publication that has been made possible by Canon U.S.A., Inc., since 1997.

There is no season such delight can bring,

As summer, autumn, winter, and the spring.

—WILLIAM BROWNE, 1591–1645

Foreword

BY ANN ZWINGER

When I was first married, we were stationed at an air force base in Florida, and I thought I'd died and gone to heaven—what could be more celestial than sunshine *all* year round? When we left four years later (and with all apologies to a beautiful part of our country), I realized I'd been bereft of seasons. I had missed the anticipation of change, missed the watchings and waitings, missed the differences between yesterday and today and tomorrow.

I grew up in the Midwest, where there *are* four seasons. I timed my childhood years by the first violets of spring along the riverbank, or the pale pink of spring beauties in the woods before the trees had leafed out to blot the warming spring sun. I loved the pussy willow catkins that burst out of shiny bud scales. Summer brought flamboyant bloom in my mother's wonderful garden; summer also brought cicadas celebrating the heavy heat that enveloped one in a mohair bodysuit and, in those pre-air-conditioning days, made sleeping a misery and one yearn for autumn. Falls were glorious; I set my autumnal clock by crimson maples and bronze oaks. I can still smell the dusky scents raked leaves sent up or the smoke of burning leaves that shimmied skyward. Winter brought spectacular sledding and snowballs, and startlingly clear days when the air was so crystalline and so sharp you could believe it would shatter if you sneezed.

Some of us may loathe heat, others detest cold, but I suspect all of us harbor that anticipation of change in the air, the smell of recognition, the recognition of change that is only part of a bigger cycle. And our memories are probably tied closely to our childhoods, when each new awareness became imprinted for a lifetime. Of course, there can also be sadness in looking back: the place along a riverbank where you picked violets as a child has disappeared or the place you did research in college is now a housing development or the hedgerows that held such a rich interior life have been cleared. The seasons of childhood may exist only in memory.

My memories are fairly domestic, of my mother's garden, of the sloping bank of our front yard that made such marvelous sledding. They did not appreciably widen until I became a natural history writer and my world suddenly opened out. Now I yearn for the first pasqueflower of spring, note in the journal the first mourning cloak, calculate the ripening of the wild chokecherries and the burgeoning of fall mushrooms. And of course, here in the West, it's the clarion gold of the aspen that marks our autumns. These recognitions and expectations, the questions and the answers, frame our concept of "home."

With this magnificent anthology of seasons, every reader's sense of place is expanded with this widest of all possible views of seasonal markers. We have the chance to see scenes out of our experience and place them in the context of what we already know about the joys of seasons. Distinct events mark each location, just like my first yearned-for pasqueflower in the Rocky Mountains, an event to be savored as unique, welcome, remarkable—always with the comfort that if you don't like this season, there's another just down the road.

This is a special book about seasons, for it portrays places, dazzlingly rich and diverse and beautiful places, forever set aside for their health and our wonderment. This book is testimony to the wisdom of choices by Nature Conservancy trustees all over the country, to the generosity of people who have cared about their local wetlands or sweeping prairie or sequestered seashore. No matter how widely I travel, I doubt that I'll ever see a maternity colony of bats in Arkansas or migrating snakes or mole crickets in Missouri, but I can visualize them from these pictures and essays.

This book begins with an end: a view of hibernation's end in Montana. We watch great blue herons courting in Maryland, prairie chickens visit a heron rookery in Texas, and owls nesting in Michigan. Without leaving an easy chair you can watch Rhode Island's Block Island birds and migrating songbirds on the Conservancy's Lafitte Woods Preserve in Louisiana. In spring, hatchings and calvings and spawnings bring out the new generations just in time for good summer feeding, leopard frogs in Utah, bison in Niobrara Valley Preserve in Nebraska, wood storks in Georgia, and Shoshone sculpin in Idaho.

Summer produces red and blue and yellow blooms on the prairies and the salt marshes of Ohio and Cape Cod. Summer is a good time to watch falcons fledge in Vermont, regal fritillaries floating above wildflowers in Pennsylvania, or seals pupping in Alaska.

Autumn brings a slowing of life, salmon returning to spawn in Oregon, all kinds of birds winding their way south through the protected Cheyenne Bottoms in Kansas. Alizarins and butterscotch and cayenne hues replace the pale lavenders and yellows of spring in a robust display of colors in Nevada. Ducks settle into winter on New York's Long Island and along Virginia's Rappahannock River. The world slows to a close with the annual Christmas Bird Count at Thousand Springs, Idaho, and winter cloaks the river on the Consumnes River Preserve in California. But inherent in the deceleration of winter is also a quickening that forecasts the breakup of the ice, snow seeping away, another year on the wing.

Part of the delight and pleasure of this book is that a walk through any of these preserves can be taken not only this year but next year and all the years hereafter because so many people have cared enough to preserve them. Wandering through this book grants us an appreciation for the stately, reliable pavane of seasons and the stability that recognition gives to our lives. Being anchored into the larger cycles of nature rededicates us to all the places we call home.

S P R I N G

One April day of sun forgives four February days of gray.

Each of us marks spring's return differently—the song sparrow's heraldic mating call early one morning, the trills from the pond of frogs at dusk, the splashes of blues and yellows and whites of early wildflowers in the still-somber woods.

Nature's spring rituals are as varied as nature itself, and the renewing cycle of a particular species often escapes our attention, unless we pay close attention. The migration of snakes. The spawning of salmon and horseshoe crabs. The nesting of storks. The wanderings of moose and grizzlies. The births of bison calves and bat pups.

Whereas winter allows us to turn inward, spring requires we look outside ourselves. We must reawaken our five senses. Find our hiking boots. Dust off field guides. Get a move on it, *for each spring moment is change.*

"To," as Thoreau said, "pass the time of day, and look freshly up . . . with spring thoughts."

The Big Sleep

Grizzlies are the untamed soul of the Rockies.
—DOUGLAS H. CHADWICK

We are not immune to hibernation's pull. Who hasn't wanted to lie down for a long winter's nap during days of hard gray skies and dipping windchills?

Many North American fish, amphibians, snakes, birds, and mammals take a snooze when the days shorten. They hibernate, or enter into a state of low metabolic activity characterized by decreased heart rate and lower body temperature that is known variously as torpidity, lethargy, and dormancy.

The most well-known hibernator among carnivorous mammals is the bear. All species of North American bears hibernate. If left undisturbed in their dens, they won't even lift their heads for the winter months. At the same time, however, bears are not "deep hibernators" and have the ability to rise from their sleep to escape danger or defend themselves.

During hibernation, bears don't eat or drink.

Their body temperatures decline, their heartbeat and breathing slow down dramatically, and they live off the body fat they built up in the fall. Remarkably, a female bear will give birth to cubs and feed them with her milk—all of this during hibernation, while she is essentially in starvation mode.

Each spring, female grizzly bears (*Ursus arctos horribilis*) and their young emerge from their snow-covered dens at high elevations of the eastern Front Range of the Rocky Mountains in Montana. It takes several groggy days for the mothers to fully shake off their winter torpor, but when hunger finally sets in, the mothers and cubs descend into the valleys and foothills for food. (Male grizzlies also appear at this time, though the sexes do not commingle and males have even been known to kill cubs.) Emaciated from their long winter's fast, some females rely on the abundance of forage at The Nature Conservancy's Pine Butte Swamp Preserve, an 18,000-acre sanctuary for grizzlies and other animals.

The mix of prairies, swamps, forests, and streams at the preserve and in the surrounding landscape are ideal grizzly habitat. The generous food supply here is so conducive to the grizzly that the females sometimes produce triplets instead of their usual twins. They also tend to give birth every two years instead of in more typical intervals of three or four years. For these grizzlies of the Eastern Front, grass, berries, carrion, and roots are the main sources of food. Come spring the adults quickly put on weight: large grizzlies here weigh between six and seven hundred pounds. Over the spring and summer, two to fifteen grizzlies will frequent the Pine Butte Preserve at any one time, though they are rarely seen by humans.

These grizzlies represent a portion of what biologists estimate to be a population of six hundred to nine hundred in the northern Rockies. When Lewis and Clark came this way, at least fifty thousand grizzlies lived south of Canada. Since then, habitat destruction and killing by people have decimated the population, and the grizzly is currently federally listed as threatened. Many conservationists and biologists fear it may vanish from the lower forty-eight states during the next century, as habitat fragmentation and destruction continue.

If so, come one spring day, a rite of spring will be lost, and the mountains will mourn. —J.K.

BABY, IT'S COLD OUTSIDE

HIBERNATION FACTOIDS

➤Among mammal groups in North America, the most hibernators are found among rodents.

➤Skunks, raccoons, and badgers all experience periods of lethargy, though they are also active during other times of the winter.

➤Raccoons may share their winter dens; though more than twenty raccoons have been reported in one den, more than one adult male per den is rare.

➤The ground squirrel is a deep hibernator. Its body temperature can fall from a normal 98 degrees Fahrenheit to as low as 34 degrees. Its heart slows from 350 beats per minute to 2 to 4 beats.

➤In the southern states, many species of aquatic turtles, such as chicken and mud turtles, hibernate on land, burying themselves underground as far away as three hundred feet from the water.

➤Some desert animals escape the summer drought by entering into a state called "estivation" that is similar in many ways to hibernation.

The Green Chorus

AMPHIBIAN COURTING, MICHIGAN

In these Michigan woods, well before the last ice breaks on the vernal ponds and the footpaths cease their mud-slogged ways, male spring peepers are rapt in song.

Northern spring peepers are thumbnail-sized frogs the color of tree bark. They're named for their sharp "peeps," which fill the damp woods and wetlands across North America each spring. At The Nature Conservancy's Jonathan Woods Preserve in March, peepers share the choral stage with chorus frogs, wood frogs, green frogs, and gray tree frogs, among others. In fact, when courtship is in full swing, these woods can be fairly deafening with frog song. Known as "advertisement calls" by herpetologists, the male frogs' songs signal their species identity, location, and genetic prowess to neighboring females. In general, biologists believe that the females are attracted to calls with lower pitch, longer duration, and greater frequency. To the females, this indicates larger, stronger, and more durable males behind the voices. In the competitive world of frog reproduction, pip-squeak peepers need not apply.

Once a female chooses a male, who has likely to this point been stationed in a tree or similar terrestrial cover, the couple repairs to water. Streams, lakes, ponds, marshes, puddles, and, in the case of Jonathan Woods, vernal (ephemeral) pools serve as the medium for mating. In some frog species, such as green frogs, males vigorously defend prime breeding pools from their competitors.

While male frogs may overwhelm the aural sensibilities in terms of their loud, nonstop calling all hours of the day and, especially, the night, female frogs lay mind-boggling masses of eggs. The egg masses, gelatinous, translucent gobs that look a little like tapioca pudding, sit on the pond bottoms, float on the water's surface, or drift while tangled in aquatic plants.

Egg numbers vary from species to species: the gray tree frog lays up to two thousand, the wood frog three thousand, the tiger salamander four hundred, the eastern newt around three hundred, and the American toad a whopping twenty thousand. As with reptiles—

sea turtles, snakes, lizards—the superabundance of amphibian egg production is an evolutionary response to environmental trials and tribulations. Not only do predators, such as fish, eat their fair share of amphibian eggs, but the habitat itself can doom an egg cluster.

In Jonathan Woods, shallow vernal pools—some no bigger than a bathtub—are fed each spring by snowmelt and rain. Leopard frogs, spotted salamanders, and other amphibians often rely on these pools for their eggs. If the pools dry up before the eggs have had a chance to hatch into tadpoles or before the tadpoles have matured enough to take to the land, then a particular reproduction effort is sunk.

Sometimes vernal pools dry up because of a low snow year, an unusually hot spring, or other natural phenomena. Too often, however, as people develop more of the woods on the outskirts of our cities and towns, these vernal pools and other wetlands get drained or paved over—a contributing factor, among many, to the alarming decline of populations of amphibians worldwide.

Back at the protected acres of Jonathan Woods, though, as spring slides into summer, the frog choruses have quieted, the warming waters are alive with squiggly tadpoles, and on the now firm footpaths the first tiny hoppers are appearing en masse.

Watch your step.
— J.K.

FROGGY GOES A-COURTIN'

A BRIEF GUIDE TO FROG AND TOAD CALLS

Among amphibians, frogs and toads are nearly the only ones that vocalize during courtship.

Northern Spring Peeper (*Hyla crucifer crucifer*)
  High-pitched peep.

Western Chorus Frog (*Pseudacris triseriata triseriata*)
  Sounds like someone strumming the small teeth of a pocket comb from middle to end with a thumbnail.

Eastern Tree Frog (*Hyla versicolor*)
  Slow, musical trill.

Green Frog (*Rana clamitans melanota*)
  "Clung!" Sounds like a plucked banjo string.

Wood Frog (*Rana sylvatica*)
  From a distance, a group of calling wood frogs sounds like quacking ducks.

Eastern American Toad (*Bufo americanus americanus*)
  Long, high-pitched trill that lasts up to thirty seconds.

Flurries of Songbirds

BLOCK ISLAND SPRING MIGRATION, RHODE ISLAND

Like flakes of snow, they flutter down upon the island during the night.
—ALFRED HAWKES, FORMER RHODE ISLAND AUDUBON SOCIETY DIRECTOR

After a long cold winter on Block Island listening to the same birdcalls day after day, bird-watchers look forward to the first new birdsong to signal that spring migration has finally arrived.

Migrant songbirds come to small, windswept Block Island to find sanctuary on their annual flight north for the summer. The island lies twelve miles off the congested Rhode Island shore and is a timeless place of open sky, treeless grasslands, crisscrossing stone walls, and dramatic clay bluffs that drop down to beaches and the pounding Atlantic surf.

Though the island is not always on the direct migratory path of these birds, migrant fringe birds appear throughout the spring. And when strong southwest winds blow, thousands of songbirds are blown off the Rhode Island coast, and the island is overrun with colorful warblers, thrushes, vireos, and flycatchers. Many birders compare Block Island's unpredictable spring migration to Christmas because each day brings a wonderful surprise—one day a birder might see the beautiful but common American redstart and the next, the extremely rare golden-winged warbler. An average spring migration on Block Island brings nine species of flycatchers, five species of thrushes, five species of vireos, thirty-two species of warblers, and dozens of other species.

Most of these migrant songbirds are returning from their winter grounds in Central and South America, and are flying to the northern United States and Canada to nest for the summer. Once they arrive on Block Island, the weary and dehydrated birds seek shelter in the island's shrub-sheltered ponds and swamps. The dense shrubs protect the birds from hungry predators, including resident northern harriers and the migrating sharp-shinned hawks, merlins, and peregrine falcons.

The secluded ponds and wetlands at The Nature Conservancy's 200-acre Clay Head Preserve are favorites of migrant songbirds and the birders who follow them. Silence greets bird-watchers wandering along the preserve's trails, until suddenly the wetlands burst into choruses of birdsong. Mixed-species flocks of small birds flurry everywhere in flashes of yellow, red, blue, green, gray, black, orange, and brown; it's nearly impossible to move your binoculars fast enough to see all the birds flying by. Each species has its own place in the flock—the warblers and flycatchers sit in the tops of the bushes, and the sparrows, towhees, goldfinches, and thrushes linger close to the ground. Then as quickly as the flock arrives, it disappears, leaving nothing but silence or perhaps a retreating birdcall in the distance. Birders can easily spend the whole day following these incredible flocks. With each encounter they can add a different bird species to their day lists.

Another remarkable place to witness the migrant birds is Nathan Mott Park. This Conservancy preserve features dead and dying Japanese black pines, an exotic species that was first introduced to the island as a landscape tree. The pines, not resistant to native diseases, are slowly dying from attacks by turpentine beetles and other insects. For the birds, this is good news; the insects are plentiful and make for a substantial meal. Birders can find birds like the black-and-white warbler and the black-throated green

warbler working over the trees for food. Unlike the flocks at Clay Head, the pace is slower here and gives birders ample time to study the birds and observe their behavior.

—S.C.

GUIDELINES FOR VISITING BLOCK ISLAND

There are approximately twenty-five miles of walking trails on Block Island that are open to the public, free of charge. When visiting this preserve or any wild place, please respect the following guidelines to protect and promote the well-being of the birds and their habitat.

1. Observe birds cautiously to prevent disturbing and endangering them.
   ➤ Stay back from nests, roosts, and feeding areas. Hide in natural cover when possible.

2. Protect the birds' environment.
   ➤ Stay on the marked trails and keep group sizes small.
   ➤ Do not move or take any plants, rocks, or animals.

3. Respect the rights and property of others.
   ➤ Stay off private property unless you have the owner's consent.
   ➤ Exercise common courtesy toward others you may encounter on the trails.

4. Promote the safety and protection of the preserves while you are visiting.
   ➤ Hunting and trapping are not permitted.
   ➤ Preserves are open only during the day; no camping or campfires are allowed.
   ➤ No bicycles or motorized vehicles.
   ➤ Keep your pets on leashes.

By following these guidelines, you will be helping The Nature Conservancy protect and maintain the wildlife and its natural habitat.

The Color of Spring

I t's like that moment in *The Wizard of Oz* when the film goes from black-and-white to color.

The springtime return of neotropical migratory songbirds is an eruption of yellows, blues, reds, and purples: yellow-throated vireo, blue grosbeak, ruby-throated hummingbird, and purple martin. Not to mention the painted bunting, cerulean warbler, American redstart, black-throated blue warbler, scarlet tanager . . . colors galore! And with the flashy males breaking into song, suddenly the dull spring woods are dull no more.

One of the premier places in the United States to observe neotropical spring migrants is Louisiana's Gulf Coast. Each March, songbirds by the tens of millions make the seven-hundred-mile dash across the Gulf of Mexico, some of them alighting in the Louisiana wetlands and woods along the coast after the exhausting journey. The Nature Conservancy's Lafitte Woods Preserve and the Audubon Society's Holleyman-Sheely-Henshaw Migratory Bird and Butterfly Sanctuary offer welcome respite for the birds.

Cheniers—the word in French means "places of oaks"—are the dominant landform here. In this case, the oaks are live oaks and they are found on ancient beach ridges, along with the other prominent tree species of this forest, the hackberry. Both species are behemoths, with the ancient evergreen live oaks growing to sixty feet, their branches radiating out from the trunk to nearly the same length. Amid these branches, the diminutive warblers and vireos could just about get lost, if it were not for their vibrant plumage.

Birders tend to have favorites for one reason or another. Black-capped chickadees, though common, delight most everyone with their looks, energy, and calls. Colors often sway a birder's tastes, such as the satiny black and bright orange of the American redstart. The prothonotary warbler looks like a Creamsicle. Indigo buntings appear the deepest of blues if the sunlight hits them just so. And then there are the warblers that have streaks and blotches and stripes and spots of color. Among these—though it is purely subjective—the chestnut-sided warbler ranks high with its bright yellow crown, black face mask, and warm chestnut-brown sides.

Both of the Louisiana preserves are so ideal for migrants that at the height of spring migration, you may see in one day most of the species of thrushes, warblers, vireos, tanagers, and grosbeaks that occur in the eastern United States. Not only are songbirds here in great and varied numbers, but so too are other birds, such as waterfowl, shorebirds, and raptors. The mudflats attract birds such as ruddy turnstones and sandpipers, while the marshes teem with roseate spoonbills, tricolored herons, and blue-winged teal ducks (more colors!). By day, Cooper's hawks and merlins hunt here, as do great horned and barn owls by night.

And lest you think all the action is in the air, you also should keep your eyes open to the land- and waterbound creatures of the preserves. River otters, glass lizards, nine-banded armadillos, striped skunks, cottonmouth snakes, and American alligators also make these woodlands and wetlands their home.   —J.K.

OUR THREATENED BIRDS

In recent decades, the numbers of migratory birds, particularly neotropical songbirds, have sharply declined. This phenomenon concerns ornithologists, conservationists, and birders alike. Reasons for the decline are complex, but habitat destruction and fragmentation in the birds' summer homes in North America and winter homes in Latin and South America and the Caribbean are incontrovertibly culprits, as is the loss of migratory stopover habitat, such as coastal areas. Many ornithologists believe that it is the loss of breeding habitat here in the United States that is the single leading factor for widespread population declines.

For example, wood thrush populations are down more than 20 percent nationwide since 1980; Baltimore orioles have declined more than 25 percent in a decade's time; and summer tanagers have dwindled 17 percent since 1980. And they are not alone. Almost all neotropical migrants are losing ground.

One of the ways you can help the birds not to lose any more ground is to help them not to lose any more ground, literally. Support international and national efforts, such as The Nature Conservancy's Wings of the Americas program to preserve bird habitat, made possible by Canon U.S.A., Inc. For more information about Wings of the Americas, see page (87) or visit the Conservancy's Web site.

Voices of the Prairie

MOLE CRICKET CHIRPING, MISSOURI

You'll likely never see a prairie mole cricket (*Gryllotalpa major*) when visiting a tallgrass prairie, because they live underground for most of their lives. But you may hear them. Their harsh chirps are common on the prairie, echoing across the open land.

At about two or three years of age, prairie mole crickets molt. Then they surface from the soil for only two reasons—courtship and mating. When the rich earth warms in the spring, male mole crickets dig a small tunnel system just at the soil's surface. The entrance is shaped like a funnel and is attached to a small oval chamber. Every evening, when dusk creeps gently over the land, the male mole crickets enter the small chamber and croon their prairie songs into the wide night sky. The grinding chirp echoes across the darkness, attracting female mole crickets, which choose and mate with the loudest males.

Mole crickets are one of the more mysterious residents of the dwindling tallgrass prairies. While deer, buffalo, and jackrabbits graze on the tallgrass prairie from above, the secretive mole crickets graze from below, on the roots of the little bluestem. Theirs is a world of darkness and earth. They are unusual insects, specially adapted to living in the rich, dark prairie sod. Their hind legs are not built for jumping, as in other crickets. Instead, their forelegs have developed into strong, formidable claws, perfectly suited for tunneling in the loamy soil.

At up to two and a half inches long, mole crickets are the largest of all crickets. These rich, brown insects match the darkness of the prairie earth except for the delicate, short gold fuzz around their throats, like small, elegant collars. Their cylindrical bodies are streamlined for moving efficiently in the round, narrow tunnels crisscrossing the prairies, and they feed on plant roots, spiders, earthworms, and other insects.

In many ways, these small, mysterious creatures are the voice of the prairie. Their songs are familiar to anyone who has ever slept under the stars and felt the warm springtime earth of the Great Plains against their back. As the prairies have been lost, the mole cricket's song has slowly died out in many midwestern towns and cities. But in special places like The Nature Conservancy's Niawathe Preserve in Missouri, the harsh chirps of several hundred calling males still sing down the night sky and revive the spirit of a place that is now largely lost to history.   —J.S.

WAH' KON-TAH'S SPIRIT

In spirit and in fact, the prairie looms large in North America's history. For millennia, plains Indians lived here. Two centuries ago, prairies were the major features of the Heartland, from Indiana to the Rockies. In modern times, however, the prairie has fallen victim to its own productivity, as people have converted its fertile soils into the world's breadbasket.

In the Osage Plains of southwestern Missouri, The Nature Conservancy has worked for more than twenty years to preserve a piece of prairie history. With the acquisition of the 875-acre Thoreson Ranch, a long-held vision is now complete. The new land connects two preserves and creates a 2,331-acre contiguous prairie named Wah' Kon-Tah after the great Osage spirit.

Visitors to Wah' Kon-Tah can see the booming grounds for greater prairie chickens and habitat for scissor-tailed flycatchers, northern harriers, upland sandpipers, Henslow's sparrows, northern crawfish frogs, badgers, and regal fritillary butterflies. The rare prairie mole cricket lives under a diverse carpet of grasses and wildflowers, including the threatened Mead's milkweed. The Conservancy periodically invites volunteers to prairie-restoration days on Wah' Kon-Tah, where they assist in stewardship activities like brush cutting and fence rolling.

With less than one percent of Missouri's original prairie remaining, large remnants such as Wah' Kon-Tah are important. Initial plans call for prescribed burns, suspension of grazing, and restoration of degraded areas. Restoring parts of Wah' Kon-Tah won't be simple, easy, quick, or cheap, but the ultimate goal is worthy: to revive Wah' Kon-Tah both in spirit and in fact.

Canopy of Color

FOREST BIRDS, HAWAI`I

Cloaked in the light mist of the East Maui rain forest, they wait, craning their necks, squinting against the pale glare in their binoculars, searching for the small, colorful, native forest birds of the Hawaiian Islands.

The bird-watchers are rewarded when a spectacular scarlet-colored `i`iwi (*Vestiaria coccinea*) flies down from the canopy to feed on the blossoming flowers of a native raspberry. The bird whirs through the dense green foliage, instantly recognizable by its loud "rusty-hinge" call and brilliant scarlet and black feathers. Until maturity, however, the `i`iwi is not so easily recognizable. Its feathers change color dramatically as the bird matures, from greenish yellow to scarlet red. The Hawaiian language has numerous words to describe the `i`iwi in its various immature phases.

The raspberry on which the `i`iwi feeds is known as the `akala (*Rubus hawaiiensis*) and is amazing in its own right. Almost thornless, it reveals the effects of evolving in an island environment devoid of predators.

Throughout the months of April and May its pale magenta blossoms and bright red or yellow fruits hang from arching branches and dab the forest understory like an impressionist painting.

During its bloom, the `akala attracts native nectar-feeding forest birds like the `i`iwi down from the upper canopy to a more comfortable viewing level. Up in the canopy, among the red pompom-like blossoms of the prominent `ohi`a lehua trees, the `i`iwi is more difficult to spot because it keeps to the interior leaves of the trees. While the `i`iwi feeds in the understory, bird-watchers can witness the bird's evolutionary adaptation: its salmon, sickle-shaped bill is a singular match for the sickle-shaped lobelia flowers from which it also feeds.

Although the `i`iwi was once abundant on each of the main Hawaiian high islands, the introduction of mosquitoes to the islands in the early 1800s has significantly impacted on its population. Feral pig populations threaten to carry mosquito populations to the higher elevations if left unchecked. These introduced mammals create wallows in which mosquitoes breed. The mosquitoes, in turn, spread avian malaria and pox to native birds, which, having evolved in isolation, are defenseless against these introduced diseases. Two weeks after a single bite from a disease-laden mosquito, an `i`iwi will lie dead on the forest floor. On the islands of O`ahu and Moloka`i, the `i`iwi is considered rare, and on the island of Lana`i, extinct. Fortunately, the `i`iwi is still common in mosquito-free areas above 1,000 meters (3,280 feet) elevation on the islands of Hawai`i, Maui, and Kaua`i.

The Nature Conservancy is working with its partners to keep feral pigs and other ungulates out of the upper elevations of the forest so that many of Hawai`i's native species can have a refuge in which to survive well into the future.

—M.R.

CULTURE AND CONSERVATION

To maintain our own beauty, we must maintain the beauty of the forest. . . .
If we cut down the forest, we cut down ourselves.

—Pua Kanahele, Kumu Hula, Halau O Kekuhi

In Hawaiian culture a long-standing relationship exists between hula dancing and the forest. Practitioners of the ancient art of hula gather from the forest the ferns, foliage, and flowers with which they make their lei and costumes. They celebrate the natural world through dance.

But the traditional relationship to the forest is also mindful of a strong conservation ethic: Take from the forest only what you need. Give back to the forest.

This important ethic has resonance in a state where the only tropical rain forests in the United States survive and where more than half of the native forest has disappeared. Local groups of hula practitioners are working to revive the Hawaiian conservation ethic—to protect the beloved wildlife that the hula practitioners have danced about for centuries.

A New Generation of Bison

BISON CALVING, NEBRASKA

April 15 often dawns cold in Nebraska's Sandhills, where snow flurries and freezing temperatures can linger into May. At this time of year, the prairie is a rustling sea of brown, giving little hint of the lush green grasses and spectacular wildflowers that will soon burst forth. Yet here on The Nature Conservancy's Niobrara Valley Preserve, an important harbinger of spring is about to arrive.

On this day each year, the preserve staff begins an annual ritual: the search for the first calf born in the preserve's herd of 250 Great Plains bison (*Bison bison*). Through the long winter, the herd has split up into small foraging groups to search the snowy, windswept prairie for exposed tufts of grass. Now, as the days warm and the snow melts, the bison gather together again into one or two large groups. The cows are gaining weight. Soon, one by one, they will move off from the herd to give birth to calves they have been carrying since the previous summer.

The calves begin to appear in mid-April each year. They arrive slowly at first, their gawky legs and ruddy coats standing out against the dark, solid masses of their mothers. Each day the preserve staff spots a few more, and by the end of May most of the herd's 180 cows have calved.

A bison calf is quite precocious, able to keep up with its mother less than an hour after birth. In the first few moments of life, however, the fifty- to seventy-five-pound calf lies helpless on the prairie as its mother hovers nearby, licking the newborn clean and encouraging it to stand with

ADOPT-A-BISON

The poet Walt Whitman called it "the great American landscape." Once the prairie filled 142 million acres, spanning portions of fourteen states. Lamentably, less than 10 percent remains today, though The Nature Conservancy is working to preserve and restore great segments of this critical landscape.

The Conservancy has reintroduced bison at five preserves across the Great Plains, including the 37,000-acre Tallgrass Prairie Preserve in Osage County, Oklahoma. Here visitors can journey back in time and experience the prairie as our ancestors did, with eight-foot-tall grasses, breathtaking wildflower displays, and roaming bison.

The Conservancy's Adopt-A-Bison program allows donors to "adopt" and sponsor any of eight bison representative of the animals at the Tallgrass Prairie Preserve. For a tax-deductible gift of $35 each year, donors can choose which bison they would like to adopt. The bison are named—Buster, Thunderfoot, Prairie Chief, Sweet Pea, Penny, Hickory, Prairie Star, and Wildfire—and their photos appear on the Conservancy's Web site.

Donations go toward tracking and researching the bison, keeping the animals healthy and disease-free, maintaining the fence and range, controlling burns, and purchasing bison calves from other herds to diversify the gene pool. In turn, donors receive an adoption certificate imprinted with their name and a photo of their bison, along with a year's subscription to *Prairie Thunder*, the quarterly newsletter that provides updates from the Tallgrass Prairie Preserve.

Adopting a bison helps the Conservancy restore the precious legacy of the prairie so that it will be here for our children . . . and their children . . . and their great-great-grandchildren. For more information about the Adopt-A-Bison program, visit the Conservancy's Web site.

gentle nudges. Rising up for the first time on shaky legs, the calf takes its first, wobbly steps as it searches for its mother's teat. The young bison will gather strength quickly, and within a few hours he and his mother will rejoin the herd.

Though the bulls prefer to travel alone, the cows and their young travel together in congenial herds for most of the year. The bulls can grow to two thousand pounds and stand six and a half feet tall at the shoulder; the cows grow to one thousand pounds. Bison can eat as much as fifty pounds of forage a day each, and they depend wholly on the prairie grasslands for food.

Once, sixty million bison thundered across the Great Plains in herds of all sizes, always grazing but always moving on, granting the land time to recover. Like fire, they were a mainstay within a balanced ecosystem. European settlers upset this balance as they slaughtered millions of bison and attempted to prevent prairie fires. By the beginning of the twentieth century, as few as one thousand bison remained, and much of the prairie they once roamed was plowed up or choked out by invading trees and shrubs.

The "sea of grass" and the immense herds of bison will never exist again, but on five Conservancy preserves these majestic animals have returned to their native habitat. At Niobrara Valley Preserve they graze a 7,500-acre enclosure, left to their own devices as nature intended. With the completion of a new 12,000-acre pasture and the addition of a second herd, nearly 20,000 acres of prairie will once again be under the hooves of the animals that helped create and shape it.

And so each spring marks an important milestone for the ever-expanding bison herds. The birth of each new calf is one more step taken toward restoring ecological balance within the Great Plains.   —J.S.

Desert Songs

NORTHERN LEOPARD FROG MATING, UTAH

The land of the Colorado plateau is not all barren rock and sand. Extraordinary pockets of water and color exist in this arid desert.

One of these places is the Scott M. Matheson Wetlands Preserve near Moab, Utah. In the springtime, brown turns to green in these warm, wet lands, and the northern leopard frogs begin to emerge from their winter hibernation at the bottom of dark, brackish ponds.

As snowmelt from the mountains upstream raises the Colorado River, the mating calls of these small frogs echo and bounce against red-rock cliff faces and into the clear, blue Utah sky. The rivers and streams that carved these canyons provide protective marshes, ponds, clear lakes, and vernal pools to harbor the frogs. Some people say that the northern leopard frog calls sound like someone rubbing a well-inflated rubber balloon; others that they sound like a motorboat or someone snoring and occasionally stopping to chuckle.

For such small creatures, their songs are loud, filling the still desert air with a cacophony. In the cool, wet places down in the canyons, among the cottonwoods and the clear streams, the air is light with breezes, and the sharp, biting scent of the desert seems a long way off. The splashes of jumping frogs mix with the clean sounds of water running over flat rocks and create the musical background for the rising mating songs.

Northern leopard frogs are typically about four inches long, with several rows of round, bordered spots on their backs. To the eye, they are smooth and sleek, but their tight skins are strangely, delicately rough, like the finest sandpaper. They live among the rustling bulrushes at the edges of streams and ponds. At one time, leopard frogs were the most common and widely distributed frogs in North America, but as they have declined across the continent, colonies have survived in the protected waters of isolated oases like Matheson Preserve.

Within days after the croaky mating songs begin, female leopard frogs begin to lay eggs. In clear, shallow waters, they attach two- to five-inch-long egg masses (containing about three thousand eggs) to the waving stems and leaves of water plants. The eggs will hatch in a few weeks, about the time the fully leafed cotton-woods begin to rattle gently in the early-summer breezes. By the time the cottonwood leaves are golden in the fall, the tadpoles are fully grown, and the cycles of hibernation and song begin again.   —L.E.

DIFFERENCE BETWEEN FROGS AND TOADS

Collectively, toads and frogs are known as anurans—tailless amphibians. All toads are frogs, though they occasionally have striking physical differences that can help you tell them apart. Frogs are found on every continent except Antarctica. Toads, on the other hand, are not found in Australasia, Madagascar, the polar regions, or Polynesia.

The skin of a toad is often thick, dry, and warty, enabling it to tolerate dry environments, and toads usually prefer to live on land. They often escape the heat of summer by burrowing into the earth, and during the winter, they protect themselves from the cold by burrowing beneath the frost line. They have short bodies and stout legs that cause them to hop instead of leaping like frogs. Many female toads lay thousands of eggs in long strings attached to surrounding vegetation.

Frogs tend to lay their eggs in clusters and to prefer moister environments than toads do. They have strong, long, webbed hind feet that are made for leaping and swimming. Their bodies are built sleek and small and their skin tends to be smooth and shiny. Their eyes bulge in large round sockets.

Snake Trek

SNAKE MIGRATION, ILLINOIS

But never met this fellow,
Attended or alone,
Without a tighter breathing,
And zero at the bone.

—EMILY DICKINSON, "THE SNAKE"

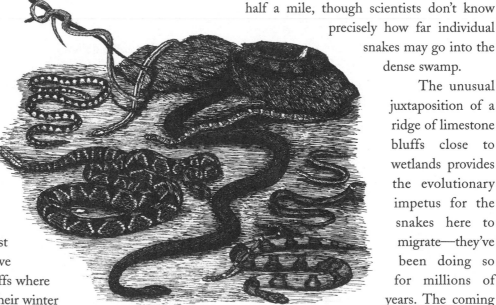

It sounds creepier than it is: huge numbers of snakes—imagine a snake stampede!—making a long, overland migration.

It's not quite that.

Nevertheless, the natural phenomenon of "snake migration" ranks as one of the more unusual you might ever witness.

Each spring, snakes in the LaRue Swamp–Pine Hills/Otter Pond area of the Shawnee National Forest in southern Illinois move from the limestone bluffs where they've denned up for their winter hibernation into the wet bottomlands where they'll summer. The distance the snakes migrate from their winter to their summer quarters is no more than a half a mile, though scientists don't know precisely how far individual snakes may go into the dense swamp.

The unusual juxtaposition of a ridge of limestone bluffs close to wetlands provides the evolutionary impetus for the snakes here to migrate—they've been doing so for millions of years. The coming

33

SNAKE SNIPPETS

➤ Worldwide, there are twenty-five hundred species of snakes.

➤ Snakes are found in a variety of habitats, including forests, prairies, deserts, streams, lakes, and oceans.

➤ Snakes likely evolved during the age of the dinosaurs from a lizard ancestor. Over time, they "lost their legs," so to speak—vestigial hip and hind leg bones exist in boas and pythons. "Legless" lizards exist today as well, but are a distinct group of animals from snakes.

➤ Although it may appear so, snakes are not fast movers. "Racer" snakes, such as the blue racer in the Midwest, move at a top speed of about four miles an hour.

➤ All species of snakes are carnivorous. The same can't be said of other reptiles and amphibians, such as frogs, salamanders, lizards, and turtles, which range from vegetarian to carnivorous to omnivorous.

➤ Females of most snakes are oviparous, which is to say that they lay eggs. However, some snakes, including the ubiquitous garter snakes, are viviparous, which means they give birth to live young.

together of bluffs, hills, meandering river, and wetlands create a slumgullion of habitats, making this the most ecologically diverse area in Illinois and one of the richest in the Midwest. Some sixty plant and animal species that are imperiled in Illinois are found here, including a manna grass, a small red damselfly, the Mississippi kite, and the Indiana bat.

But the snakes—their diversity, rarity, and numbers —are what make LaRue Swamp–Pine Hills/Otter Pond so remarkable. Cottonmouth, green, garter, black rat, earth, mud, ringneck, speckled king, timber rattler, flat-headed, scarlet, and copperhead, among others, are concentrated here. Three of Illinois's four kinds of venomous snakes are here. The swamp harbors the largest population of cottonmouth snakes ("water moccasins") in the Midwest. A Conservancy scientist recalls seeing 125 of the venomous cottonmouths along the base of the bluff on a warm spring day back in the 1950s.

While the kinds and populations of snakes here are significant, their numbers appear to be down considerably from this observation in the 1950s. A gravel road divides the bluffs from the wetlands, and in less ecologically enlightened times, according to a U.S. Fish and Wildlife Service biologist, people used to come out in the spring and fall and kill snakes, either by shooting them or by running over them with their cars. Another devastating factor that continues today is the illegal collection of snakes. "We call it 'snake-napping,'" says Raymond Smith, USFWS biologist. "And we will prosecute snake-nappers when we catch them." The entire 277,000 acres of the Shawnee National Forest are closed to snake collecting.

These days, the gravel road is closed to traffic at the height of the migration, for two months in the spring, and again in the fall. People can walk the two-mile-long road during the migrations to observe the snakes. Smith says that on a warm day in early March, you might see a dozen snakes. The Conservancy biologist Max D. Hutchison says that though he's been to the area countless times, he has only seen a few snakes at one time slithering across the road to disappear into the swamp.

While this certainly constitutes no stampede, witnessing this snake trek is nonetheless a thrill and, perhaps, for a few of us at least, a thrill with a bit of the willies attached.   —J.K.

Living Fossils

HORSESHOE CRABS SPAWNING, DELAWARE

As spring warms to summer each May, the horseshoe crabs swim ashore along the sandy beaches of the Delaware Bay, just as they've been doing for over 250 million years.

Easily recognized by their hard brown shells, numerous claw-tipped legs, and long, spiked tails, horseshoe crabs are often known as living fossils. Children walking Delaware's beaches with their parents are commonly both frightened and fascinated by the odd, flat crabs scrabbling along the sand.

Despite their name, horseshoe crabs don't look very much like crabs. They are more closely related to spiders and scorpions than to crabs. Female horseshoe crabs, which are larger than the males, can grow to two feet wide and weigh as much as ten pounds. They can look like large, brown hubcaps waddling from the surf.

As the water warms in spring, the horseshoe crabs begin to move from the deep waters of the ocean and the bay toward the shores to spawn. When the moon hangs full and lights the beaches with a wash of pale light, the horseshoe crabs scramble from the ocean and build small nests in depressions in the sand. Some females can lay as many as 90,000 eggs in one season, with an average of 3,650 tiny eggs in each nest. In places along the coast of the Delaware Bay, the crabs are so deep and thick along the beach they blanket the sand. Visitors cannot walk without treading on the hard brown shells. They are a tumbling carpet of movement, their dark shells drying in the rising sun.

As the horseshoe crabs come in living waves across the beach, the shorebirds are close behind. More than a million birds converge along the shores to feast on the eggs of the largest concentration of spawning horseshoe crabs along the Atlantic Coast. Red knots and ruddy turnstones are the most numerous. And sandpipers, plovers, avocets, stilts, and oystercatchers skitter along the waterlines and feed on the exposed horseshoe crab eggs.

They probe the sands with their spiked bills and eat only the vulnerable top layer of eggs. The shorebirds stop here on their annual spring migration from South to North America. They must eat and rest to finish the long trip north. They dine on a rich diet of horseshoe crab eggs in preparation for the end of their migration. Scientists estimate that a small sanderling will try to double its body weight quickly by eating one horseshoe crab egg every five seconds for fourteen hours a day.

They make unusual partners: the dipping, graceful shorebirds with their familiar dance before the waves and the lumbering, ungainly horseshoe crabs tumbling from the water in the warming nights of spring. It is an ancient relationship, as timeless as the oceans and the bays, a moving cycle of life along the remaining undisturbed beaches of the Delaware Bay.   —C.B.

HORSESHOE CRABS

With its hard brown shell, hidden underbody, numerous claw-tipped legs, and long pointy tail appendage, there really isn't anything else that looks much like a horseshoe crab. The species native to Delaware (*Limulus polyphemus*) lives in bays and on the continental shelf along the western shores of the Atlantic Ocean, stretching from Maine to the Yucatán. The largest population of horseshoe crabs in the world occurs within the Delaware Bay and the adjoining continental shelf.

DID YOU KNOW? Horseshoe crabs have been around for a very long time. The earliest horseshoe crabs inhabited earth for at least one hundred million years prior to the arrival of dinosaurs. That's about three hundred million years ago, which makes the horseshoe crab one of the earth's oldest living animals.

Horseshoe crabs are prized for their use in medical science, including research on human eye function, development of suture materials and wound dressings that accelerate healing and relieve pain, and use of a clotting agent in the crab's blue blood to test new medicines for the presence of harmful bacteria.

On average, a female will deposit in the range of twenty thousand eggs at a time, though some have been known to lay up to ninety thousand. During the spring migration season, at least twenty species of shorebirds feed on horseshoe crab eggs during their singularly important Delaware Bayshores stopover, replenishing their depleted energy resources before completing the long journey north to their Arctic breeding grounds.

The horseshoe crab is actually more closely related to spiders and scorpions than to true crabs.

Bats Are Mothers Too

BAT MATERNITY COLONIES, ARKANSAS

Bats are mothers too.

Witness the female vampire bat of the American Tropics, who weans her baby over a period of months by gradually changing its diet from breast milk to a combination of milk and blood (fed mouth-to-mouth) to blood alone, taking the pup, once it can fly, along on her nocturnal feeding. Mother bats of all kinds even carry their flightless young to relocate them if their roosting site is endangered—no small feat, given that a newborn can weigh one-third as much as the mother.

One of the most remarkable aspects of bat motherhood is the formation of maternity, or nursing, colonies. Some contain thousands, if not millions of bats. One such colony is found in Arkansas, in the Ozark Mountains, in a dank and dark cave whimsically known as Blue Heaven.

The maternity colony here, a modest population, is composed of Ozark big-eared bats (*Corynorhinus townsendii ingens*), a federally endangered species. The bat's range has historically been Oklahoma, Arkansas, and Missouri, though this subspecies is now believed extirpated from Missouri. In Arkansas, the population of Ozark big-eared bats was estimated to be two hundred in 1992. Maternity colonies of bats are just what you'd expect: aggregations of female bats with their young. While both genders of many species of bats share hibernation caves in the winter, when spring arrives the sexes part ways. The females congregate in caves, where they give birth and wean their young. In most species of bats, the female has only one baby—an evolutionary adaptation to flight, biologists believe, since being weighted down with several fetuses would reduce the endurance and agility a bat needs to feed in the air.

Female Ozark big-eared bats roost communally in the pockets of cave ceiling that get the warmest, some up to 60 degrees Fahrenheit. Maternity caves for other bat species can get even warmer, upward of 100 degrees. The warm temperatures of maternity caves are a result, in part, of the body heat given off by each bat. And therein hangs a clue as to why bats form such aggregations. The collective heat accelerates the maturation rate of newborns. A North American bat that hibernates during the winter needs stores of fat to survive. A newborn must be able to fend for itself quickly so it can begin voraciously eating to prepare for winter's torpor. Ozark big-eared bats, born in May or June, are on their own by summer's end. Maternity bat caves are incubators, of sorts, giving newborns the edge they need to survive.

Young bats face not only seasonal perils but dangers within the nurseries themselves. A flightless baby bat that loses its grip on the cave ceiling or its mother's fur (it has especially large feet and first fingers to minimize this mishap) often does not last long on the cave floor, as predaceous insects and fish (if there's water below) quickly devour it. A variation on the fish-eat-bat relationship is found in several Arkansas caves: bat guano is the basis for the food chain supporting the Ozark cave fish and other organisms, both aquatic and terrestrial.

Nationally, bats have more species on the federal endangered species list than any other group of mammals. Habitat destruction and vandalism have decimated bat populations, and in Arkansas alone three of the sixteen species of bats found here are endangered.

Thus, the decline in bats has affected entire cave ecosystems, illuminating in the pitch black of a cave the biological interdependence of life.   —J.K.

BAT HOUSES

If you've wondered about those birdhouses without the hole that hang on the sides of garages, trees, and fence posts, they are most likely bat houses. Bat houses provide artificial roosting sites for bats and help conserve a group of animals that has long been misunderstand and persecuted by humans.

Despite bats' reputation for carrying rabies, less than half of one percent do, and fewer than ten people in fifty years have contracted rabies from North American bat species. Three-quarters of the one thousand species of bats in the world eat insects; a single North American little brown bat can catch six hundred mosquitoes in just one hour. Other kinds of bats are vital to pollinating and dispersing seeds in rain forests.

While conservation of bat habitat is the best way to preserve this remarkable mammal, bat houses placed around your yard are also beneficial. Not all species of North American bats will utilize bat houses, but many will—a single chambered house about the size of a bluebird box can accommodate fifty bats!

Construction plans and instructions about how and where to place bat houses on your property are readily available in bookstores, on the World Wide Web, and from conservation groups, such as Bat Conservation International.

The Chattering of Little Birds

RED-COCKADED WOODPECKERS, SOUTH CAROLINA

Once you could find the red-cockaded woodpecker (*Picoides borealis*) throughout the Southeast, from Texas to Florida and north to Missouri, Kentucky, and Maryland.

No more.

The red-cockaded woodpecker, more commonly called RCW, lives exclusively in mature longleaf pine forests. Unfortunately, these trees have been cleared in much of the South, making this woodpecker an endangered species.

The RCW is small (about eight inches long), with a large white cheek patch. It is considered a ladderback woodpecker, a group of birds named for the black-and-white ladder patterns across their backs. The red cockade, a tiny patch of red feathers above the white cheek patch of the adult male bird, is often not visible. But in places like South Carolina's Sandy Island, between the Waccamaw and Great Pee Dee Rivers, RCWs still thrive amid the longleaf pines, and you won't have any trouble spotting their homes, or cavities.

Most woodpeckers make their cavities in dead trees. The RCW lives only in live trees, specifically open stands of mature pines that are greater than eighty years old, and avoids places with a dense hardwood understory. Its ideal tree has a fungal disease—red heart—that softens the wood and makes excavation easier. And when you consider that the RCW has to work for months and sometimes years to excavate a proper roosting cavity, you'll understand its need for a tree softener.

On Sandy Island and elsewhere, this woodpecker has a fairly complex way of life. It lives in a family group, which consists of the breeding male and female along with helper birds, generally the male offspring. The group stays together, roosting in clusters of trees, where each member has its own roost cavity. Birds tend to make their cavities between twenty and fifty feet above ground, below live limbs. Most groups have several

40

cavities under construction at any given time, with some closer to completion than others. Often there are several cavities in a single tree. Sometimes they abandon, or stop working on, cavities. So not every cavity you see has a bird in residence.

To spot an active cavity tree, look for small holes, called resin wells, above and below a cavity entrance. The sap flow from resin wells gives the tree a candle-like appearance and helps deter predators, including snakes. The cavity itself starts out as small upward tunnel extending about six inches or more into the tree, and eventually becomes a chamber within the heartwood of the tree as large as ten inches deep and five inches wide. A smooth, reddish appearance to cavity trees and other pines within the RCW's territory is a result of the birds' foraging for insects beneath the surface of the bark.

There are perhaps twelve thousand RCWs left in the United States—about one percent of the population before European settlement. The bird no longer exists at all in Missouri, Maryland, and New Jersey.

The remaining populations are fragmented into isolated island populations. Find a forest filled with RCWs, and you are probably in a healthy stand of mature longleaf pine trees.

This is certainly the case on the northern end of Sandy Island, at the Conservancy-managed Sandy Island Preserve. Most of the pines here are greater than one hundred years old. In thriving longleaf pine communities like these, the chattering of these little birds remains a delight in the morning air.   —J.B.

SAFE PLACES FOR WOODPECKERS

Since most of the remaining longleaf pine forest in South Carolina—about 369,000 acres—is on private lands, local conservationists have worked hard to encourage landowners to manage these forests to benefit the RCW. The latest success is the "safe harbor" habitat-protection program.

Under this innovative idea, landowners statewide have been invited to improve habitat for the bird and, in doing so, win protection from incurring added legal liability for endangered species that move onto their land. Established not long ago, the program already has fifteen initial participating landowners—representing 84,000 acres and 150 woodpecker colonies. By early 1999, more than 23,000 additional acres of land in North Carolina were enrolled, including golf courses, a horseback-riding club, and private forest owners.

The program was spurred by a coalition: the Environmental Defense Fund, state officials, landowners, forest-products companies, the U.S. Fish and Wildlife Service, and other conservation groups. Next, conservationists acting on behalf of the RCW will try to secure financial incentives to help landowners with the cost of protecting large tracts of mature trees and administering prescribed burns.

Quick-Change Artists

SHOSHONE SCULPIN SPAWNING, IDAHO

In the entire world, there is only one known place to find the elusive Shoshone sculpin (*Cottus greenei*). These tiny, inconspicuous fish are found only in the sixty-mile Thousand Springs Reach of Idaho's Snake River.

The tadpole-shaped Shoshone sculpins live in the river's clear springs, and grow no larger than two inches long. These feisty fish change color like chameleons—turning blotchy olive, brown, and gray—to blend into their background. They can transform themselves from light to dark and back again in seconds to camouflage themselves from their predators: hungry mink, otter, trout, and the sharp-eyed heron and kingfisher.

Because they lack swim bladders, the organ that makes most fish buoyant, the sculpins cannot float. When they stop swimming, they sink to the bottom. They spend most of their time lazing on rocks at the river bottom or lurking among vegetation, making occasional short forays out to munch on diatoms and daphnias and other small planktonic morsels.

During the breeding season, from May through July, the male sculpin selects a crevice under a rock and coaxes a female to wiggle in upside down and lay her eggs on the crevice ceiling. He fertilizes the eggs and then guards them until they hatch. During this period, he's a watchful and pugnacious protector who's even been known to charge a human hand if he perceives it as a threat to the nest.

The sculpins are found only in the most pristine of the river's remaining springs, including the three spring creeks at The Nature Conservancy's 400-acre Thousand Springs Preserve. The preserve borders the meandering river for two and a half miles, and its creeks pour nearly a thousand cubic feet per second of pristine water into the river. Several thousand sculpins live in the preserve's waters.

The sculpins' presence in other parts of the river is a sign of clean water and an important indicator of the health of the Snake River Plains aquifer, the source of drinking water for tens of thousands of people in southern Idaho. In the past, sculpins have been threatened by trout-farming methods that added excessive nutrients to the river. Local agriculture and the hydroelectric industry also have altered many of the thousand springs, threatening the sculpins' homes. In recent years, however, these industries have worked to reduce their effects on the river. The feisty sculpin population in the river is currently stable and, for now, it has the clean, pristine waters it needs to survive.

—P.H.

WHY FISH CHANGE COLOR

Deception is everywhere in the fish kingdom: it is the key to underwater survival. One of the most common tricks is changing color.

Some fish change color to avoid predators. They camouflage themselves against their backgrounds to hide. Others use what scientists call "disruptive coloration"—eye-like marks on their tails, for example, that divert predators away from their heads to a less vulnerable part of their anatomy. And many poisonous fish use bright color as a warning to predators to stay away.

When fish are spawning, both males and females turn ostentatious colors to signal that they are looking for mates.

And when males want to guard their territory, many fish flare their fins at the edge of their territory to warn off possible intruders. In combative encounters, fish will often change color yet again: losers turn pale, while winners brighten to signal victory.

Night Song

The sounds of insects fill prairie nights with their moonlight serenades. Crickets, katydids, grasshoppers, and cicadas are musical wizards.

Just as frogs and owls can be identified by their night songs, so too can insects. And while grasshoppers sing by rubbing their legs together, other members of the night choir, the katydids and crickets, use their wings. The katydids and crickets produce sound by means of a ridge-and-file system. They call by scraping the fixed ridge on the edge of their forewing against the file on the underside of the other wing. Grasshoppers have several ways of producing sound. The most common way is by scraping the teeth-like structures on their hind legs against a vein on their outer wing covers.

But why, when the sun begins to set and the night sky covers the prairie, do the insects sing?

Generally, only male insects sing; a few female katydids will respond to the male call with a click. Calls vary among courting calls, territory calls, and aggressive calls. The competition among some of the evening singing insects is fierce, and the loudest singer attracts the females.

On any given night on The Nature Conservancy's 25-acre Ames High Prairie in Iowa, these amazing insects fill the night air with hums, clicks, and chirps. In early August, prairie enthusiasts meet on the prairie to listen.

Ken Shaw, a retired zoologist from Iowa State University, has led the Night Sounds on the Prairie field trip for years. The remnant prairie of gently flowing hillsides bordering a woodland offers an entirely different feel at night than during the day. Gone are the floral distractions—the showy flowers and waving tall grasses—and all that remains under the cloak of darkness is the song of the insects.

During these night walks, fifteen to twenty species of crickets, katydids, grasshoppers, and cicadas can be identified by sound alone. Crickets, katydids, and grasshoppers don't live long. They make their debut in spring as nymphs, with small wings and immature reproductive parts. Over the summer they go through several molts, reaching adulthood in early fall, when their wings and reproductive organs mature and they are able to mate. While some insects begin calling in late June or early July, it is in early fall, when their wings and reproductive organs are fully mature, that the orthopteran orchestra reaches its summer crescendo.

On the next warm summer night, go sit on your porch and listen as nature's choir fills the night sky with its song.

—J.S.

HILL PRAIRIES

Ames High Prairie is known for its remnant patches of hill prairie—prairie that grows on sloped land where there is little soil coverage over limestone and sandstone bedrock. Because hill prairies are located on such unarable slopes, many have been spared cultivation.

Hill prairies, also called goat prairies, are covered with native grasses, including Indian grass (*Sorghastrum*), big bluestem (*Andropogon gerardii*), and blazing star (*Liatris aspera*). Their favored locations are sunny southern slopes surrounded by oak, ash, hickory, and maple trees.

Today, hill prairies are threatened not only by habitat destruction but also by an unexpected source: the eastern red cedar (*Juniperus virginiana*). In the past, this coniferous tree was confined by natural fires. Since fire is less prevalent today, the red cedar is spreading over many hill prairies, forming a canopy that overshadows the prairie grasses.

Most remaining hill prairies are in private ownership, including Ames High Prairie. Its 25 acres of high rolling land overlook the wooded Squaw Creek Valley and support dry-mesic prairie and a rare butterfly, the wild indigo duskywing (*Erynnis baptisiae*). Situated behind Ames High School, it is frequently used as an outdoor-education laboratory by the students. Recently Ames High Prairie was designated as a state preserve to afford it the highest protection status in the state.

Moose Country

MOOSE VIEWING, NEW HAMPSHIRE

Moose—immense, beguiling, and goofily majestic—are naturally drawn to deeply wooded and watery places like The Nature Conservancy's Fourth Connecticut Lake Watershed in northern New Hampshire. Here, along the Canadian border, the watershed and its spruce and fir forest provide food, water, shelter, and solitude for these magnificent animals.

In spring and summer, the moose (*Alces alces*) lounge in the shade, wade knee-deep in water, and munch on herbaceous plants surrounding the bog. Young moose travel quietly through these woods with their mothers. Even in the shadowy light, their light brown baby fur stands out against the darker chocolate color of the protective mothers.

Henry David Thoreau described the moose as "singularly grotesque and awkward." His opinion aside, these immense animals—some stand as high as seven feet at the shoulder, with racks of antlers as wide as a man is tall—are undeniably majestic. As the biggest member of the deer family, moose are the second-largest land animals in North America. Adult males can weigh more than half a ton.

They might look awkward, but moose move with surprising grace. Their long, lanky legs serve them well in deep water and snow and help them navigate the obstacles of the forest. Their anatomy is ideal for living in the North Country. Their elongated, bulbous noses help them feed easily in water, and are lined with tiny blood vessels that warm freezing air. Their two-layer winter coats retain body heat and block the cold, even on the most frigid days.

BRAKE FOR MOOSE

The moose are back. Today, thousands of moose thrill tourists and terrify motorists throughout New England.

Unfortunately, as the numbers of moose increase, so do incidents of accidents involving cars and moose. And when these accidents do occur, they can end in disaster. Most moose weigh over a thousand pounds. Because of their height, they often land directly on the windshield when hit, and car-moose collisions can be fatal to the car's occupants. The moose fare even worse: several hundred moose are killed by cars in New Hampshire alone each year.

There is no known solution to this problem. Experienced moose-country drivers follow road signs, stick to the speed limit, and take special caution when driving at dawn and dusk, since at these times visibility is poor and the moose are most active.

The moose can also be dangerous to people on foot. No matter how docile a moose might look, it is never wise to get too close. Though moose are one of the few wild animals that will stand still and let humans near them, any moose can be dangerous at any time. It is particularly dangerous to get between a mother and her calf. Mothers are extremely protective and might attack. And it is equally wise to avoid moose during the fall rutting, or mating, season because the males may attack anything moving within their turf.

In the spring, the moose shed their shaggy winter coats in favor of lighter summer fur, and avoid the heat by limiting most of their activities to dawn, dusk, and cloudy days. Their antlers, dropped before winter, now grow back quickly—as much as one inch per day. During these warm months, the moose spend much time eating to put on extra pounds in preparation for winter. An average moose can eat twenty-five to fifty pounds of vegetation a day.

From spring to early fall, the moose are attracted to roadways by the road salt left over from winter snow-removal crews. They emerge from the woods to lick up the salt and chew on mud from puddles alongside the road. One New Hampshire roadway, Route 3, is so popular with them that it's been nicknamed Moose Alley. Though moose-car collisions are a danger in this area, tourists are still drawn to the lovable moose, and they line up in their cars to see the animals strolling leisurely down the road.

We are lucky to still have the moose; it was once approaching extinction in much of this country. In the 1960s, the moose population was thought to be down to seventy-five individuals in all of New Hampshire. Now, thanks to regulated management of the moose herd and improved forest management, the New England moose population has increased to thousands. The moose has made an amazing comeback.

Hikers along the Conservancy's steep and rugged trail into Fourth Connecticut Lake are rewarded with frequent glimpses of moose in their native habitat. The moss-cushioned trail winds through conifer trees and patches of flowering wood sorrel. It leads to the headwaters of the Connecticut River, a ten-acre moss-covered bog surrounded by clumps of wild-flowers. Here, amid one conifer-covered hill after another, the moose find a quiet and shady sanctuary, a safe home in natural habitat.   —P.H.

American Colonialists

Now in large circles they seem to ascend toward the upper reaches of the atmosphere; now, they pitch toward the earth; and again, gently rising, they renew their gyrations . . . the most beautiful evolutions that can well be conceived.

—JOHN JAMES AUDUBON, JOURNAL, NOVEMBER 1831–MARCH 1832

All newborn birds are ugly ducklings.

It takes a leap of faith to imagine featherless, crone-like, and spasmodic hatchlings one day emerging into graceful swans, resplendent orioles, or even delightful chickadees.

Some ugly ducklings in the bird world, however, stay so. Thus is the lot of the wood stork.

One of the biggest birds in North America, weighing some seven pounds and standing four feet tall, with a black featherless head and long, thick beak, wood storks (*Mycteria americana*) were nicknamed flintheads by early European settlers in the American South. The term refers to the birds' resemblance to the firing mechanism on a musket. Actually, the head of the young wood stork is covered for a time in white down, but as the bird matures the feathers fall out, leaving a bald adult.

As the only species of the worldwide stork family found in the United States, wood storks are great American colonialists: at the turn of the century, wood stork colonies numbered into the tens of thousands of pairs, and such colonies were commonplace in the South. Today, such large colonies are

PLATE 247

John James Audubon's Plate 247 in his masterwork *The Birds of America* is labeled "Wood Ibis (*Mycteria americana*)." Early naturalists in America mistakenly thought the wood stork was a kind of ibis, incorrectly grouping it with a common family of similar-looking birds found throughout the South. Instead, the wood stork is the sole American representative of a family known as Ciconiidae. Be that as it may, Audubon likely first encountered wood storks around 1820 on a trip to the American South. He dated his painting of the wood stork "April 17," and it is believed to have been done in 1821.

In his journal, Audubon wrote evocatively of wood storks, of their graceful flight and deadly skill at dispatching baby alligators. He painted the birds as well; his technique was to mount fresh kills with wire and then set them to canvas. Audubon himself shot many of the 435 species in *The Birds of America*. And while bird lovers today might find this difficult to understand—after all, isn't the Audubon Society named after him?—one has to remember that in the early nineteenth century this practice was not considered antithetical to being a naturalist, or an enthusiast of nature.

gone because of habitat loss. The wood stork has been listed as an endangered species since 1984. Today, there are an estimated five to seven thousand breeding pairs of wood storks in the southeastern United States.

One site with a healthy local population of wood storks is the Harris Neck National Wildlife Refuge on the Atlantic Coast of Georgia. Hundreds of wood stork pairs nest here each spring, among stands of gnarled, stunted black gums draped with Spanish moss and surrounded by alligators and the omnipresent hum of mosquitoes.

Here, in the heat and humidity of the South, you can witness one of nature's great collectives, a condo in the trees: the nests of wood storks and other waders, such as ibises and herons, fill the branches so close they nearly touch. The storks' nests themselves are bulky, three feet in diameter, and tend to be found in the highest reaches of a tree, secured to a horizontal branch. Made of sticks and whitewashed in excrement, a typical nest has two to four eggs, laid in March, shortly after the birds migrate from their wintering grounds in southern Florida.

By summer the chicks have hatched and are a fed a steady diet of regurgitated fish, snakes, turtles, baby alligators, rodents, and plants from the omnivorous parents. After about a month, the hatchlings' wing feathers are well on their way to maturity. Weeks later, the young wood storks fledge and begin the household clamor that accompanies adolescent milestones in any species. Both the activity and the noise level in the rookery escalate.

Standing on shaky legs at nests' edges upward of one hundred feet high in a tree, maniacally flapping their wings, the white-downed youths look comic and even dangerous to themselves and their fellows. And they're loud. "Grunts, loud and deep-throated; shrill squeals, incessant and angry; bellowing, coughing, deep wheezing, bleating," recounts one ornithologist of a wood stork colony during the fledge.

Eventually, the young leave the nest. Once airborne, the wood stork sheds all of its earthbound homeliness. The sight of wood storks in flight inspired the naturalist-painter John James Audubon to rhapsodize in his journal of "the most beautiful evolutions that can well be conceived."

So remember Audubon—who had a good eye for beauty—if you ever have an opportunity to see a stationary wood stork up close and gaze into its black eyes: when the stork is on the wing, there is a swan inside.

—J.K.

SUMMER

Cicadas know summer. Their pulsating buzz ushers in summer twilights in which the heat does not slacken.

By summer, some wildflowers are getting "leggy," their stems and branches elongating, with colorful blooms fewer and farther between. But other flora is just coming into its own now: the showy pink of Tennessee coneflowers, black-eyed Susans, and butterfly weeds of the prairie, the myriad grasses and sedges along a salt marsh. The tall grasses of the Great Plains are waist-high, while the understory of eastern forests has become so tangled up in green as to be nearly impenetrable. As Joseph Wood Krutch once observed of summer, "If nature is ever purely vegetative, it is now."

But wait. Summer is also fur seals pupping in Alaska, peregrine falcons fledging in Vermont, sharks feeding in the shallow waters of a California slough, regal fritillaries and other butterflies in Pennsylvania, bobcat kittens in Colorado, and sea turtles nesting in Florida.

Yet summer's swoon comes too soon, marked by early-fall migratory birds already southbound, and the cicadas ceasing to sound.

The Rings of Time

Time is but the stream I go a-fishing in.
—HENRY DAVID THOREAU

Canoeing down the tea-colored waters of the Black River, drifting by gnarled bald cypress trees decorated with resurrection ferns and gray Spanish moss, you find that time slips away. In June, the river is a visual and auditory delight, with bright yellow prothonotary warblers (some people call them swamp canaries) zipping in front of you, their cheery calls ringing in the air. If you are lucky, you may spot an otter eyeing you from the bank. More than likely, the wary creature will dismiss you with a snort and belly-slide into the river, leaving only a trail of bubbles in the black water.

The Black River originates in Sampson County and flows sixty-six miles through southeastern North Carolina before emptying into the Cape Fear River fourteen miles above Wilmington. The Black River takes a winding course, frequently dividing and forming many small islands and sloughs.

As one of the cleanest rivers in eastern North Carolina, the Black River seems relatively untouched by time and shows little evidence of lasting human disturbance. The river harbors many species that have disappeared from elsewhere in the Cape Fear Basin, including rare fish species such as the Santee chub and broadtail madtom, and the Cape Fear spike, a globally endangered freshwater mussel. The river's broad floodplain provides a wildland corridor for black bears, bobcats, and river otters and is a critical breeding area for neotropical migratory songbirds such as the prothonotary warbler and yellow-throated vireo.

But the river's ancient trees are the ones grabbing today's headlines. A classic black-water river swamp-forest borders the river, dominated by bald cypresses, black gums, and red maples. The oldest bald cypresses are easily recognized by their flat storm-blown tops and their huge buttresses, which measure fifteen to twenty feet in diameter at the point where they emerge out of the dark waters.

While people always suspected that the bald cypresses were old, no one knew just how old until a dendrochronologist in the mid-1980s measured the trees' growth rings. His findings astonished everyone: some of the trees are at least 1,650 years old. The first year of life for one of the trees began in A.D. 364.

These aged cypresses are standing today because the older they get, the more gnarled they get. From the late 1800s to 1924, the Black River was an important thoroughfare for steamboats traveling between Wilmington and Point Caswell in Pender County. The boats transported loads of cypress shingles and barrels of pitch, tar, and turpentine produced from longleaf pines. Loggers spared the ancient cypresses standing today, deciding they would have made poor lumber because they were hollow and twisted.

Escaping the ax and withstanding the pounding rains and winds of countless hurricanes, these trees have outlived others of this swamp. At one time, colorful Carolina parakeets ate the cypress seeds and nested in the trees' cavities, while ivory-billed woodpeckers chattered overhead. Today the former is known to be extinct and the latter presumed to be extinct in the United States.

While, sadly, these incredible birds are gone, black bears still den in the trees and parula warblers nest with Spanish moss gathered from the branches. And we can visit this place, on the Black River, where we measure out our lives with tree rings. —I.L.

THE TREES' KNEES

Bald cypress trees (*Taxodium distichum*) take fifty years or so to show their "knees."

When you consider that the bald cypress can live hundreds, even thousands of years, this is hardly surprising.

The knees, if you've ever been in a bald cypress swamp, poke out of the inky water around the trees' trunks and look somewhat like termite mounds. They are peculiar root growths and are known technically as pneumatophores. The spongy wood of the knees helps the trees' roots get much-needed oxygen, which is in short supply in waterlogged soil. Those bald cypresses that live hundreds and thousands of years may be surrounded at their base by dozens of knees.

Phantom Cats

BOBCATS, COLORADO

Claw marks on a tree. A guttural growl. A paw print.

All signs of the elusive bobcat.

Bobcats are mostly nocturnal, and wildlife watchers usually have to settle for seeing only fleeting signs of their existence.

Tracks are perhaps the most common sign that a bobcat has been nearby. Bobcat tracks are somewhat similar to those of a coyote but are more rounded and show no claw marks—a characteristic of the retractile claws of most cat species.

If you are able to track this cat, which is slightly larger than the domestic house cat, with adults weighing between eleven and thirty-one pounds, you may find its den. Dens are typically hidden in rock crevices, caves, hollow trees, or logs and sometimes in thickets.

If you're lucky, you may hear a bobcat's sharp cries during the mating season, typically in March and April, although bobcats may breed at any time of the year. Their litters are small—two or three kittens—and the offspring begin fending for themselves when they're about nine months old. As summer comes into full bloom in June in the Colorado backcountry, bobcat kittens will tentatively venture out short distances from their dens for a look around.

Often confused with the Canadian lynx, bobcats have shorter fur with more distinct spots, shorter ear tufts, and smaller, less hairy feet. They also have a longer tail—albeit bobbed—than the lynx, and they sport dark bands across the front legs. Their bobbed tail is black-tipped, with spotted or streaked fur that is grayish in winter and reddish in summer.

Bobcats, also known as wildcats, are stealthy hunters that depend on surprise rather than an all-out chase. Although they will feed on almost any prey, including small mammals, small birds, amphibians, crayfish, and even deer given the right opportunity, their favorite menu item is a cottontail rabbit.

Found throughout North America, bobcats in the

American West prefer pinyon-juniper woodlands and montane forests and usually live in the rocky, broken terrain of the foothills and canyonlands. Ever shy, they avoid farmland, unbroken grasslands, and densely populated areas.

In Colorado, they inhabit The Nature Conservancy's Aiken Canyon Preserve, one of the largest high-quality foothills ecosystems along the Front Range. And they are one of an impressive number of mammal species found at the spectacular Phantom Canyon Preserve, which harbors rugged, bobcat-pleasing granite canyon country carved by seven miles of the North Fork of the Cache La Poudre River.

Scientists also believe that these cats inhabit Conservancy preserves along the San Miguel River, one of the few remaining rivers in the western United States that still functions naturally. The San Miguel represents one of Colorado's most precious ecosystems, made even more so by the presence of these elusive phantoms of the feline world.   —M.H.

NORTH AMERICAN CATS

Bobcats (*Lynx rufus*) are one species of cats, or members of the family Felidae, found in the contiguous United States. Their range is extensive, from coast to coast, as far south as Mexico and as far north as Canada.

A close relative, the lynx (*Lynx canadensis*) overlaps the territory of the bobcat in the north. Primarily, as its Latinate epithet indicates, the lynx is found in Canada.

The mountain lion (*Felis concolor*) ranges throughout the American West; an isolated population, the Florida panther, is found in southern Florida. The mountain lion's size is eclipsed by a rare predator in the United States, the jaguar (*Felis onca*). Once found throughout the American Southwest, the jaguar today lives primarily in Mexico and is a rare resident, if not only a visitor, to the border states.

The status of several other borderlands wildcats is similar: ocelot (*Felis pardalis*), margay cat (*Felis wiedii*), and jaguarundi cat (*Felis yagouaroundi*).

Film Loaded?

The great American landscape painter Thomas Moran came to Wyoming in 1871 with a government survey team en route to Yellowstone. Moran often wandered the backcountry in the company of William Jackson, a photographer, both men chronicling what they saw in their respective mediums. Later, Moran's paintings and illustrations and Jackson's photos would appear in popular magazines, awing the American public, most of whom had never been west of the Mississippi. Their work helped influence Congress to create the first national park in 1872 at Yellowstone.

Today at The Nature Conservancy's Tensleep Preserve in north-central Wyoming, nature photography remains alive and well, more than one hundred years after early photographers such as Jackson first captured the quintessential western landscape of this state in image.

The 8,500 acres of Tensleep Preserve are nestled in the foothills of the Bighorn Mountains, bisected by two deep canyons. Here, vast horizons surround you, offering sublime sunrises and dramatic sunsets. Ponderosa pine forests, lush meadows, and winding streams traverse the property. Wildlife abounds, with pronghorns, black bears, elk, golden eagles, and more than 120 other bird species. Wildflowers, too, grace Tensleep: bluebells, lupine, Indian paintbrush, cinquefoil, and Rocky Mountain bee plant. In short, the photographic possibilities are inexhaustible for the amateur shooter at Tensleep.

While Jackson and professional nature photographers such as Ansel Adams used large-format cameras that were cumbersome to transport into the backcountry, most amateurs and even professionals today prefer the 35 millimeter. Versatile and durable, the SLR (single-lens reflex) 35 mm offers the photographer the most options for the variety of situations he or she may encounter in the wilds. It should be noted that photographers disagree as to what the optimal equipment is to bring along as they go in search of their subject. Plan for every contingency and thus bring a host of lenses, tripods, flashes, speeds, and kinds of film? Or go light, with a couple of lenses, maybe a tripod or monopod, and a variety of film types, including black-and-white. No matter what equipment you bring, in a landscape such as Tensleep, you'd be advised to plan for at least three kinds of photographic situations: landscapes, portraits, and action.

Wildlife photography, too, comes with issues of wilderness etiquette. Is hanging out at a watering hole in a parched landscape ethically acceptable if your presence dissuades even one wild creature from slaking its thirst? What about getting that shot of the grizzly bear—worth life and limb to you or it?

The oft-used backcountry edict to leave only footprints and take only photos is problematic if your visit has included trampling wildflowers and spooking wildlife in search of the photograph that will wow the folks back home. So remember that the only thing better than a great photograph to remind yourself of the splendor of places like Tensleep is the memory that in your visit you did no harm. —J.K.

NATURE PHOTOGRAPHY 101

Professional nature photographer Lynda Richardson has had her work appear in *Nature Conservancy* magazine, among numerous other publications. Here are a few tidbits of advice from one of the pros:

➤ Research your subject: Before heading out in the field, study up on the natural history of the place and the wild things found there. Not only will this give you a better appreciation of what you might see, it will also help you decide what camera equipment you might need.

➤ Tripod: You need a sturdy one with "quick-release plates" and a "ball head." Quick-release plates attach to different camera bodies, and a ball head allows you to swivel the camera to take shots that are horizontal, vertical, or anything in between. Regarding "camera bodies": pros and serious amateurs often have at least a couple of cameras with them; typically, one is loaded with a slow-speed film and the other, fast so that they can react to different photographic situations. (You can also load one with color film and the other with black-and-white.)

➤ Film: In general, films with slower speeds, 64 and 50, for example, are best for nature photography. They give you the richest colors. More often than not, these are the speeds of film the pros use. That said, 100-speed film provides more versatility in low-light situations in which you need to use a fairly fast shutter speed—say, photographing elk at dawn. Finally, fast film, such as 400, has its merits, especially if your subject matter requires you to use a telephoto lens and fast shutter speed, and your light source is low. Imagine here your 300 mm lens on a tripod, pointed at dusk at a mountain lion that has just crept out of the tree line across the valley.

Pretty in Pink

TENNESSEE CONEFLOWERS BLOOMING, TENNESSEE

*I have great faith in a seed. Convince me that you have
a seed there, and I am prepared to expect wonders.*

—HENRY DAVID THOREAU, *Faith in a Seed*

At first glance, the parched rocky earth of the central Tennessee cedar glade appears unyielding. Found in openings of eastern red cedar forests, the glades mimic the severity of small deserts and suffer extremes of light, temperature, and moisture. Shallow dry soil, chipped gray limestone, prickly cacti, and unearthly-looking grasses dominate the barren landscape. Until summer. Then this harsh habitat bursts with some of the most beautiful and colorful floral displays in Tennessee.

In June and July, when the heat of summer is thick in the air, the cedar glade comes alive with vibrant hues. A kaleidoscopic array of yellows, purples, and especially pinks floods the dry glade, transforming the barren land into an oasis of color.

One flower in particular stands out. Once thought to be extinct, the Tennessee coneflower (*Echinacea tennesseensis*) was rediscovered by chance in 1968 by Elsie Quarterman, professor of plant ecology at Vanderbilt University, and her graduate student Barbara Turner, along the side of a road in Davidson County near Nashville.

Today, that roadside is the Mount View Cedar Glade Preserve, a 9-acre Nature Conservancy site that protects one

AN IMPORTANT DISCOVERY

Like too many species in the plant and animal world, *Echinacea tennesseensis,* the Tennessee coneflower, once held a dubious distinction: missing and presumed extinct. Unlike other lost species, however, this particular brand of flower experienced a serendipitous rediscovery that greatly improved its chances for survival.

It began in the summer of 1968. "We were out on the glades together doing research and we decided to take a different route home," says Vanderbilt University professor Elsie Quarterman, who, along with her graduate student Barbara Turner, happened across several fields of an unidentified daisy-like flower. "Driving along we noticed a pink composite, which was unusual since most glade plants are not that color." Intrigued, the pair pulled over to take a sample.

Back in the lab, Quarterman and Turner compared their newly acquired sample with other specimens, strongly suspecting they had uncovered the missing Tennessee coneflower. Quarterman recalls that it was easy to identify the plant's genus, *Echinacea,* but that the species was another matter, since no lab specimens of *E. tennesseensis* were available for comparison.

In the end, the botanical world would have to wait a few weeks to confirm the authenticity of the plants. But it was worth it. As soon as his teaching schedule would permit, Ronald L. McGregor, the undisputed authority on coneflowers, visited that roadside with Quarterman and other colleagues. After he examined the plants, Quarterman remembers, "He told me, 'Well, now you've got another cedar glade endemic.' It was very exciting."

In 1979, the Tennessee coneflower became the first Tennessee seed plant to receive federal listing as an endangered species. Quarterman says, "I was very definitely satisfied about that." And for good reason. Left unnoticed and unprotected in rapidly developing central Tennessee, the coneflower might have become *truly* extinct.

of only five native populations of Tennessee coneflowers left on earth.

At Mount View, the coneflowers spring up from the edge of the cedar grove to the center of the glade, where the tallest and heartiest plants hold the sunniest spots on the open terrain. Befitting their family name, Asteraceae, the bright magenta coneflowers look like delicate stars atop thin green wands (*aster* is Greek for "star"). With the aura of a mirage, life on the glade in summer seems to emanate from the coneflowers. Insects buzz around them, heat rises off the bedrock in visible waves, and everything from the grasses to the forest line appears to fall away from the flowers themselves.

Glade life is not easy, but Tennessee coneflowers are perfectly adapted to it. First and foremost, they can take the heat. On summer days, with the sun and humidity magnified by the exposed limestone of the glade, it can be a sweltering 120 degrees at the base of the plants. For survival, the coneflower is taprooted, meaning it has a deep root that grows down into the soil and limestone cracks to retrieve water. Indeed, most glade species have either taproots or shallow roots. Taprooted plants, such as the coneflowers, can survive in the hot sun, whereas those with shallow roots, such as glade cress and stonecrop,

bloom early in the spring, when the glades experience flooding.

Another of the coneflower's heat-survival mechanisms is the array of tiny, translucent hairs along its stem. This fuzzy layer helps prevent the sun-loving plants from excess transpiration—a plant's version of sweating—and therefore allows it to retain more water.

Preserving the glades themselves remains the surest way to safeguard the coneflowers and the other rare and unusual flora there. But other methods are being employed as well. For example, in the effort to save the species from extinction, selected nurseries and botanical gardens have been allowed to legally propagate *E. tennesseensis,* which is protected by both state and federal law.

Mount View is one of the few cedar glades that have survived the onslaught of urbanization in central Tennessee. Such glades—which occur only in central Tennessee, northern Alabama and Georgia, and southern Kentucky—were considered wastelands by many people and were often used as dumping grounds, as pastures for small animals, and, later, as development sites. Few people realized that many of the plants growing in these desolate-looking patches were found nowhere else in the world—until the rediscovery of the coneflower.   —A.M.

Floating in the Summer Haze

Near Harrisburg, Pennsylvania, each summer brings the promise of hot days, warm evenings, and the return of the spectacular regal fritillary butterflies.

By mid-July, the wide grassy fields of Fort Indiantown Gap Military Reservation blaze with color as the bright orange-and-black butterflies float in the summer haze. This is an unlikely sanctuary for a shining brood of butterflies, but the military reservation hosts what could be the fritillaries' last strong colony in the eastern United States.

Every year, as the regal fritillaries (*Speyeria idalia*) slowly emerge from their chrysalides, they instinctively search for the nectar found in the colorful blooms of thistles, bee balm, milkweed, mountain mint, and butterfly weed. The flower smells of summer are the scent of life for the butterflies. In the mornings, they float lazily among the grasses after the sun burns off the early mists. The males appear first each summer, and when the females emerge two weeks later, the mating searches begin.

Since the males live for only about a month, they search quickly for mates. They patrol for females with slow, steady flight, their wide, bright wings tipped gently against the breezes. The summer air is filled with the silent flights of dipping, gliding butterflies.

BUTTERFLIES AND MOTHS

Butterflies and moths both belong to the order of insects known as Lepidoptera, meaning "winged with scales." When any of the four broad wings of these creatures are touched, a powdery substance rubs off on the fingers. Under a microscope, the apparent powder is revealed to be masses of overlapping, shingle-like scales that have a characteristic color, shape, and pattern for each species.

All lepidopterans hatch from eggs and become worm-like larvae called caterpillars. But butterflies and moths have certain general distinctions. Butterflies have long thread-like antennae with a swollen club at each tip. Moths do not have clubs; the tips of their antennae may be pointed, feathery, or spur-like. Butterflies typically have brightly colored wings that do not fold over the body when at rest. Moths are usually dully colored, with wings that do fold against the body.

Butterflies are usually most active in the daytime (diurnal). Moths, on the other hand, are usually nocturnal or crepuscular (flying at dusk or in the dim morning hours). There are, of course, exceptions to these generalities. Some moths fly during the day; and some so-called butterflies, such as the small grass-loving skippers, don't neatly fit into either category.

Their wings are rounded, delicate laceworks of orange and black and white, and their thin bodies seem touched with velvet.

When July melts into August, the males begin to disappear and the females rest in the tall grasses to prepare to lay eggs. They walk delicately among the plants, moving carefully across the leaves and stems, and lay single eggs on various plants. By the time they are finished, cooling breezes in the night air are already beginning to hint of winter. The eggs hatch before winter comes, and the tiny caterpillars nest among the drying grasses and falling leaves until spring, when they emerge to feed exclusively on violet leaves. Thus begins the short, bright life of a regal fritillary among the flowers and the grasses and the warm touch of summer.

Though these butterflies were once abundant from Massachusetts to Virginia, the last forty years have seen the numbers of regal fritillaries diminish. Today, Fort Indiantown Gap Military Reservation is likely the last viable colony outside the center of the regal fritillaries' range in the Midwest. At the reservation, the butterflies go about their lives while tanks, armored personnel carriers, and trucks maneuver across much of their grassland habitat.

The Pennsylvania National Guard has been working with The Nature Conservancy to preserve and manage the grasslands with prescribed burns and to protect the habitats that support this fragile colony of regal fritillaries. The Guard has also reduced the amount of tank activity in the area and encourages local volunteers to construct food plots for the butterflies on formerly restricted military territory. Every summer, Conservancy staff and National Guard personnel hold several guided walks so that people can see the butterflies in flight.   —L.K.

Sweet the Smell of Summer

PRAIRIE WILDFLOWERS BLOOMING, OHIO

It is the height of summer, when heat rises from the ground in shimmering waves and buzzing cicadas give voice to the season. This is when the unique lands of the Edge of Appalachia Preserve in Ohio are bright with blooming wildflowers. From the second week of July until the end of August, the prairie plants are in their glory.

Plants called rattlesnake master and rough blazing star light the land with color and life. Visitors to the prairies at this time of year can walk through forests of wildflowers, with hundreds of butterflies floating lazily around their heads. Swallowtails, skippers, and great spangled fritillaries drink the nectar from purple coneflowers, black-eyed Susans, and butterfly weed. The dry air is sweet with the smell of summer and heat and the rich scent of prairie earth.

Butterfly Milkweed

Black-Eyed Susan

Eared False Foxglove

The big bluestem grasses grow thick and high, and in some years the prairie dock, a plant with a bright yellow face like a sunflower, grows taller than most men. Visitors who duck beneath this blooming canopy are rewarded with another layer of beauty. Orchids, blazing stars, and sunflowers thrive among the thick stalks and turn their bright faces toward the sun, but visitors must bend closer to the earth to see them and touch their soft petals.

These glades, located just seventy-five miles east of Cincinnati, are treasures of color in the rich, forested hills. In many ways, the plants that bloom and thrive and light the land here among the tree-shaded hollows are gifts from the Great Plains, a few hundred miles to the west. They are remnants of an earlier time when glaciers crushed the land and then retreated.

These hardy plants were pulled into a water- and heat-ravaged landscape. When the soils were stripped away and the forests were gone, these prairie plants were the only life that could thrive here, and in thriving, they rebuilt the rocky soils. Today, the lands are carefully managed and fire is used to keep the glades open and protected from invading trees.

These glades are bright pockets of color and life in the midst of Appalachian rolling hills and oak forests.

This is where the East and the West begin to mix. This is where pioneers slowly left their familiar lands of woods and streams to reach the broad expanse of the Great Plains. These prairie wildflowers still bring the hint of things to come for travelers going west. The land will slowly widen and open up until it almost seems that the prairie swallows the sky. And here, on the edge of Appalachia, the beauty of the Great Plains does not seem so very far away. —C.B.

SEED EFFORT AIDS OAK OPENINGS

To promote the preservation of native vegetation in the Oak Openings region of northwestern Ohio and neighboring Michigan, The Nature Conservancy has entered into an innovative relationship with local commercial greenhouses. Seeds from about thirty species of native grasses and forbs collected from local preserves are being germinated and sold by greenhouses for planting on private property.

One of the participating greenhouses has established a new nursery specifically for the production of native seeds that will be sold for planting. Another greenhouse will raise immature perennial, annual, and woody plants to market to wholesalers, retailers, landscapers, and other large-volume purchasers.

Each plant package contains an identification tag with information about the Oak Openings and the Conservancy. By increasing the abundance of native plants on private lands, the Conservancy staff hopes to improve the overall health of the ecosystem and help combat the intrusion of nonnative species. The project is successful on many levels because it helps maximize preserve resources and expands the world of partners working for the benefit of the Oak Openings.

A Tale of Seals

FUR SEAL PUPPING, ALASKA

*The numbers of birds and marine mammals feeding here, to a person
familiar with anything but the Serengeti or life at the Antarctic convergence,
are magical. At the height of migration in the spring, the testament
of life in Bering Sea is absolutely stilling in its dimensions.*

—BARRY LOPEZ, *Arctic Dreams*

A long time ago, as local legend goes, Igadagax, the son of a tribal chief, was hunting when a great wind swept his kayak far out to sea. For hours he struggled to keep afloat in the storm. When the wind finally subsided, he found himself in a dense, swirling fog. Through it, he could hear the calls of birds and the bellowing of seals. The sounds grew closer, and suddenly shore and cliff loomed before him. On the land were millions of seals. The creatures were so thick he had to search for a long time before he could land. Igadagax stayed there a year, gathering seal skins, and then returned home, bearing proof that he'd found the island of the seals.

Igadagax had found the Pribilof Islands, five volcanic isles clustered in the middle of the Bering Sea. In 1786, a Russian sailor named Gavril Pribylov, upon hearing native stories of a fur seal island, spent weeks searching for it, intent on making a fortune in seal pelts. Since Pribylov's discovery, the seals, once numbering well into the millions, have nearly been exterminated twice.

Today, some one million northern fur seals (*Callorhinus ursinus*), roughly 74 percent of the world population, still return annually to their breeding grounds on St. Paul and the other Pribilofs.

The northern fur seal is well adapted to the frigid

PRIBILOF ISLAND STEWARDSHIP PROGRAM

The Pribilof Island Stewardship Program is assembling a strong force for preserving the beauty, native culture, and livelihood of the Pribilof Islands: local young people. The effort—supported in part by The Nature Conservancy—combines science and traditional ways to involve native youths in stewardship and cultural activities.

Each summer, a group of youths attend stewardship camp, where they learn about their island ecosystem from elders, each other, and scientists. Older students assist the scientists with such activities as data collection, census taking, beach monitoring, and disentangling fur seals from discarded fishing nets and other debris. During an annual subsistence harvest, campers also learn storytelling and crafts as well as traditional seal-hunting methods.

Summer camp is often just the first step for participants in the Stewardship Program. Since its creation in 1991, several former campers have gone on to pursue college degrees in natural sciences or related fields.

Over the long term, the ethic being fostered by the Stewardship Program has far-reaching potential—from raising conservation awareness in the Bering Sea islands to providing native youths with the knowledge and skills that are essential for a seat at the management table. This is stewardship not only of an incredible natural wonder but of a people and their future.

waters of the Bering Sea. Unlike some marine mammals, the fur seal depends on its dense fur coat—rather than layers of fat—for warmth and insulation. At three hundred thousand hairs per square inch, the fur seal's coat is virtually impenetrable by water.

The seals remain at sea most of the year, returning to land to breed. Many travel as far as seven thousand miles to return to their breeding grounds on the Pribilofs. Visitors can first see seals in late April and early May, when the adult bulls come to establish their territories. Averaging 450 to 600 pounds when they arrive, the bulls may lose as much as 25 percent of their weight, going up to seventy days without eating in order to defend their territories and their females.

The females arrive in late June to late July, around the same time as the subadult (three- to five-year-old) males. The females congregate in harems around the adult bulls, typically twenty to sixty cows around each bull. The young males gather on the rookeries' edges in areas of the beach called haul-outs. Mature females average 90 to 110 pounds, making for one of the largest size differentials between the male and female of a mammal species.

Usually within forty-eight hours of their arrival, the females give birth to one pup each. Only four to seven days later, they mate again, usually with the bull that controls the territory. Over the next few months, the cows will make multiple feeding trips to sea. These forays last from three to eight days, during which time the cows travel great distances. Some are known to have traveled as far as 180 nautical miles away. Meanwhile, the pups remain on the beach, sleeping and playing. Because fur seal mothers will nurse only their own pups, a youngster will not feed again until its *own* mother returns. The mother identifies her offspring by the sound of its bleat and by smell. Nursing continues through October, when seals of both sexes and all ages begin to leave the islands, and into mid- to late November.

While this spectacle of wildlife seems evidence of a system in perfect ecological health, in truth the Bering Sea is in trouble. Indeed, the northern fur seal is listed as "depleted" by the Marine Mammal Protection Act. Though still one of the richest ecosystems in the world, the Bering Sea has suffered severely from commercial whaling and fishing, pollution, and introduced species. These human-caused stresses may have aggravated natural climatic changes.

For now, however, Igadagax's island of the seals endures.
                                                              —E.D.

Songs and Sightings

If you want to see birds, you must have birds in your heart.
—JOHN BURROUGHS

Very early on summer mornings, a solitary figure wanders across Wisconsin's rolling prairie grasslands, listening for birdsongs, spotting bird nests, and taking copious notes.

Yet this is no ordinary bird-watcher.

He is an atlas observer, doing his part for an innovative five-year project called the Wisconsin Breeding Bird Atlas (WBBA). The goal is to document for the first time the actual breeding status, distribution, and abundance of all bird species found in the state.

This survey comes just in time. With the loss of much of Wisconsin's prairie habitat has come a corresponding decline in many grassland bird species. Three of Wisconsin's native grassland birds have been extirpated, and another fifteen to twenty are declining. Many of these species are dependent on a treeless landscape for their survival—landscapes that are virtually gone in the area of Wisconsin's historic prairie grassland range.

The Nature Conservancy and other conservation groups are supporting WBBA at the Blue Mounds Prairie Heritage Area, an approximately 30,000-acre grassland landscape in southwestern Wisconsin. Here, birds are already part of the Conservancy's conservation strategy, and surveying provides valuable information about species diversity and changes in bird populations.

Surveying varies over the summer months according to the birds' behavior. In June, the sound of birdsong can be deafening as they sing to mark their territories and attract mates. In early morning, the atlas observer surveys the entire area, identifies species by song, and searches for nests. In July, when the birds concentrate their energies on building nests in the prairie grasses, their singing tapers off except for very early in the morning. Through the end of August, the observer carefully records all singing males, occupied nests, and adult birds carrying nesting material and food for their young.

The hope is that such rare birds as the loggerhead shrike, the upland sandpiper, and the short-eared owl will be spotted here. Though they have been seen on these lands in the past, they have not been spotted recently and their numbers are in decline throughout the state. Other birds of interest are the bobolink, northern harrier, eastern meadowlark, and grasshopper sparrow. The area is also a haven for other species that are declining rapidly throughout the country, including the Bell's vireo and Henslow's sparrow.

These species do well here because much of the vast Blue Mounds area is used in compatible ways. The Conservancy owns two preserves within the area. The land's rolling topography has helped, causing many farmers to keep their land in pasture instead of growing crops in rows. Finally, a federal program has successfully encouraged farmers to keep their land out of production. Though most of this land is not native prairie, the nonnative grasses still provide critical food and shelter for these bird species.

Hopefully, with bird-surveying projects like this across the country, coupled with conservation efforts, these birds will continue to fill the prairie skies with clamorous birdsong for many summers to come.—P.H.

ATLAS PROJECT

The Wisconsin Breeding Bird Atlas (WBBA), sponsored by the Wisconsin Society for Ornithology and supported by private groups and public agencies, is just one of many state breeding-status bird-atlas projects across the country. Their goal is to compile comprehensive atlases revealing the breeding, distribution, and abundance of all bird species in their state. The atlases will then provide information to researchers, birders, conservation groups, landowners—anyone who is concerned about the current status of our birds.

The projects are typically dependent on both paid experts and knowledgeable volunteers who can identify birds either by sight or by birdsongs. The surveying is called "atlasing," and each atlas observer samples an assigned block of land. In Wisconsin, for instance, WBBA has hundreds of volunteers, each monitoring an area three miles by three miles. In all, each corner of Wisconsin will be sampled by the end of the five-year project.

If you enjoy bird-watching and want to develop your field skills while at the same time contributing toward scientific and conservation efforts, contact your local birding groups to see if your state has its own atlas project.

Where the Land Meets the Sea

SALT MARSHES, CAPE COD

*I had that sense ... in the presence of the withdrawing tide, that we live, or survive,
at the indulgence of some great global courtesy, a net of seemliness of manners
thrown over the earth's blind and wrathful forces, a primitive lust of the sea for the land
checked by some overriding decorum that we call regularity of the tides.*

—ROBERT FINCH, *Common Ground*

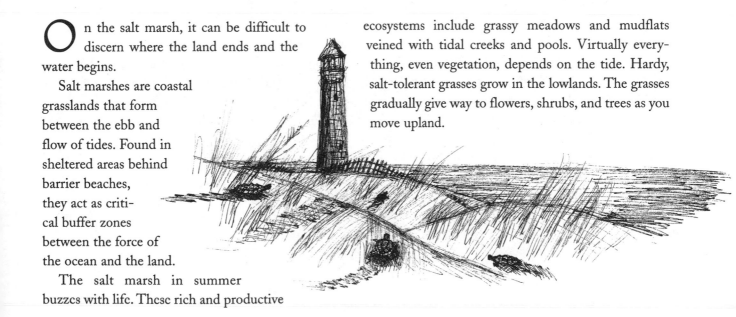

On the salt marsh, it can be difficult to discern where the land ends and the water begins.

Salt marshes are coastal grasslands that form between the ebb and flow of tides. Found in sheltered areas behind barrier beaches, they act as critical buffer zones between the force of the ocean and the land.

The salt marsh in summer buzzes with life. These rich and productive ecosystems include grassy meadows and mudflats veined with tidal creeks and pools. Virtually everything, even vegetation, depends on the tide. Hardy, salt-tolerant grasses grow in the lowlands. The grasses gradually give way to flowers, shrubs, and trees as you move upland.

One practical way to explore the salt marsh is by canoe or kayak. Paddlers entering the marsh follow marsh creeks and navigate their way around stands of cordgrass. As the mainland approaches, the vegetation grows thicker, with marsh grasses brushing both sides of the boat. In the vegetated marsh, the ground becomes firmer from the tangled roots of the cordgrass. The water becomes brackish as the marsh meets the land, and the cordgrass gives way to the shorter, thicker salt meadow hay, or salt grass. Grasses gradually change to fleabane, sedge, and cattails before the trees start to close in.

The Nature Conservancy's Boat Meadow Preserve in Cape Cod, Massachusetts, is an excellent example of a classic New England salt marsh. The preserve encompasses 126 acres of wetlands alongside a sandy upland peninsula. In the summer, paddlers can drift on the tides, experiencing the salt marsh at water level, where they can see, hear, smell, and feel the marsh through the eyes of its inhabitants.

Here, young northern diamondback terrapin hatchlings make their way through purple sea lavender and seaside goldenrod toward the sea. The trip may take the young turtles up to eleven days. Along the way they will encounter many predators, from herring gulls and ospreys to foxes and coyotes, before reaching the safety of the open water.

Meanwhile, floating in the brackish waters of the salt marsh, the adult northern diamondback terrapins forage for fish, crustaceans, mollusks, and succulent marsh plants. They are the only turtle to inhabit the salt marshes of Massachusetts, and this is the northernmost location where they can be found.

The salt marsh shelters all kinds of life. It serves as a nursery for a myriad of young fish and shellfish. The piping plover, a threatened species, nests here in spring and summer on exposed coastal barrier beaches and wind-scoured blowouts. Along the channel bottoms, lobsters, spider crabs, hermit crabs, and horseshoe crabs scurry. Mollusks and sea stars anchor themselves to the banks of the marsh.

Out past the sea of grasses, beyond the sand spits and mudflats, juvenile common and roseate terns fly around their parents, testing their young wings on the warm August breezes. This is the season when they learn how to fish, though, more often than not, the young birds will try to steal a fish from their mother's beak instead of fishing on their own. The mother lands on the spit with a fresh catch in her beak, only to be immediately surrounded by fat, young terns vying for the prize. Soon these birds will depart for the warmer winter climates of Central and South America, leaving the marsh eerily quiet. But for now, in these last hazy days of August, they congregate gregariously on the salt marsh spits and flats before their long flight south.

—P.H.

TERRAPIN FACTS

The northern diamondback terrapin (*Malaclemys terrapin terrapin*) gets its name from the distinctive diamond pattern of rings and ridges on its shell. It is found along the Gulf Coast and along the Atlantic Coast from Florida to Massachusetts. Cape Cod is the northernmost point where this species has been found.

The northern diamondback terrapin requires unique habitat for its survival. It is the only turtle species to inhabit salt or brackish tidal marshes, mudflats, shallow bays, and tidal estuaries. Each summer for millions of years, the female terrapins have also used nearby sand dunes or coastal banks for laying their eggs.

Currently there are only thirty known nesting locations in Cape Cod for the threatened terrapin. Unfortunately, many of these upland nesting areas are becoming rapidly developed as prime real estate. The Conservancy is working to protect the terrapin's natural habitat and to limit further dense coastal development that may threaten the existence of these striking turtles.

Pull of the Wind

PEREGRINE FALCON FLEDGING, VERMONT

*Like the seafarer, the peregrine lives in a pouring-away world of no attachment,
a world of wakes and tilting, of sinking planes of land and water.
We who are anchored and earthbound cannot envisage this freedom of the eye.*

—J. A. BAKER, *The Peregrine*

In the skies of Vermont, a remarkable drama is played out as a peregrine falcon, talons extended and wings partially closed, moves in on his prey. With the grace and ferocity of a true predator, he plunges straight down, reaching speeds of 200 miles per hour. He strikes just once, in midair, killing his quarry instantly.

It is one of nature's most unforgettable sights. But how do the peregrines (*Falco peregrinus*) develop this extraordinary skill and precision?

Most, it turns out, learn it from their parents. And one of the best places to observe young falcons leaving the nest, or fledging, is on the red pine ledges of Deer Leap, a four-hundred-foot cliff at the south end of Hogback Mountain in Bristol, Vermont.

Since 1987, the site has produced twenty-nine fledglings, more than any other place in Vermont. It may not sound like many, but for a bird that was once entirely eliminated in the eastern United States by DDT poisoning, this represents an encouraging comeback.

Peregrine falcons annually return to Deer Leap's steep cliffs in late February and early March. The peregrines are born in April, as Hogback Mountain comes alive with the early colors of spring. The delicate hatchlings weigh little more than an ounce and stare out at the world from large black eyes.

GIVING PEREGRINES A CHANCE

Less than twenty years ago, because of widespread DDT insecticide use, there were no peregrine falcons left east of the Mississippi. Today, DDT is banned in the United States and the peregrine is making a comeback in many eastern states, including Vermont. Unfortunately, the bird now faces another serious threat: human disturbance.

People are drawn to the peregrines and want to observe them. However, during courtship and mating season, the birds are highly sensitive to human activity and are easily disturbed by any activity near their nests.

Activity can distract the falcons, prevent them from reproducing, or even cause them to abandon the nest for good. Disturbances can also cause eggs to roll off the ledge, chicks to fall out of the nest, or fledglings to have a flight accident. And if the adults are spooked and leave the nest for any period of time, the eggs or chicks could freeze.

The mating, nesting, and fledging period for the falcons runs roughly from late February through the end of summer. During this time, The Nature Conservancy asks all observers to please respect restricted-area signs—all falcon observation should be from a distance.

A tiny pink beak and talons are the only spots of color on their downy white bodies.

But the little birds grow quickly. Soon darker feathers begin to appear in their downy coats. Already feeling the pull of the wind, the youngsters spend hours flapping their wings in the nest, furiously practicing for their first solo flight.

The big day arrives in late June or early July, when the air is warm and the forest floor is carpeted with lady's slippers. Tentatively, the young birds—now officially called fledglings—take their first, terrifying flights. Reluctant to venture too far from the security of the nest, the vulnerable youngsters stop often at nearby trees or perching sites and usually return home for supper.

With the daring and resilience of children, however, they persist and quickly catch on. In just a few short weeks, they are ready to begin hunting and caring for themselves.

Adult peregrines find many ingenious ways to introduce their fledglings to the thrill of the hunt. Often they begin by transferring food in midair or flying above their young offspring and dropping prey in front of them.

As the fledglings become better fliers, their parents lead them on rapid chases and then step aside, allowing their children to finish the hunt.

By August, the youngsters are on their own, traveling increasingly farther to hunt and forage. Eagerly, the birds test their newfound power, looping, diving, and rolling in the sky, building strength for their impending journey south for the winter.

For those on the ground, it is a deeply hopeful sight. Slowly, with each new fledgling, a magnificent, independent spirit is returning to the Vermont skies. The peregrines have been sorely missed.   —B.D.

Gift of the Glaciers

PRAIRIE CELEBRATIONS, MINNESOTA

All those fall afternoons were the same, but I never got used to them.
The whole prairie was like the bush that burned with fire and was not consumed.

—WILLA CATHER, *My Antonia*

It has been called a gift of the glaciers. Some twelve thousand years ago, the Pleistocene ice sheet disappeared in North America, giving rise to a great ecosystem stretching from Manitoba south to Minnesota, the Dakotas, and Iowa: the northern tallgrass prairie. Here, for centuries, bison and elk grazed, wildflowers bloomed, and birds found sustenance in watering places called prairie potholes.

Once vast, bursting with life and vibrant colors, and extending into the distance as far as the eye could see, the prairies rested on a thick black soil that would prove their undoing. Settlers, eager to make homes in the New World, began tilling the soil and planting crops. By the early twentieth century, the tallgrass ecosystem was a tiny fraction of its former self.

The Nature Conservancy's Schaefer Prairie Preserve is one remnant of the estimated eighteen million acres of the northern tallgrass that once covered a third of Minnesota. Today, less than one-tenth of one percent of the original tallgrass prairie that greeted the state's pioneers remains.

Located less than an hour west of downtown Minneapolis, the Schaefer Preserve has been owned and managed by the Conservancy since 1967. Its former owner, Mrs. Warren Leonard, played as a child amid its beautiful wildflowers and grasses tall enough in late summer to "hide a horse," as she described it.

Her mother's family acquired the property in 1881. Fortunately, Mrs. Leonard's parents, the Schaefers, never plowed the land; they used it only for hay. As a result, the 160-acre preserve harbors more than 245 species of plants, including the small white lady's slipper, Sullivant's milkweed, and the native Hill's

RETURN OF THE NATIVE

At several sites in Minnesota, The Nature Conservancy is hastening the return of native plants to the northern tallgrass prairie by working to eliminate invasive plant species. Volunteers and staff are removing woody species like European buckthorn and juniper, which dominate understory vegetation and reduce biodiversity. To control leafy spurge, the biggest threat to native grassland flora, certified staff members are using a strict schedule of mowing and prescribed burning.

Reseeding is also helping to restore native prairie grasses and forbs. Prairie Restorations Inc. (PRI), a Minnesota company that does landscape restoration as well as seed production, produces such prairie plants as big bluestem, smooth aster, purple prairie clover, and stiff goldenrod. PRI is called upon by government land managers, private businesses, and individuals who want native plants. The process could be described as "progress in reverse"—turning the plowed lands of today back into the prairie of yesterday.

thistle. Schaefer Prairie is one of a few locations in the state where visitors can hear the ascending and descending whistle of the upland sandpiper, or the "pump-handle" creaking of the American bittern.

It takes many people to nurture this land. Conservancy staff and volunteers regularly cut and remove invasive weeds such as Canada thistle and woody species like buckthorn and aspen. Trained fire crews conduct prescribed burns within a secure system of firebreaks. These carefully controlled fires simulate the wildfires—set either by Native Americans or lightning—that sustained the tallgrass prairie and its attendant biodiversity for centuries.

On the preserve's "old fields," staff and volunteers have been gradually restoring the landscape by dispersing millions of seeds each spring. Then, in the early summer, seedlings are planted—as many as fifteen hundred in 1998.

For many, the highlight of the year is Minnesota Prairie Day each August. For five consecutive years, visitors have come here from across the state to celebrate the state's prairies with lectures and a tour of the preserve. Visitors learn about natural history, gardening with native plants, environmental education, landscaping and horticulture, and prairie protection and restoration.

As a prime example of the state's most critically endangered habitat, Schaefer Prairie also attracts visitors young and old for research and field trips. Seeds harvested here were used to create the "reconstructed prairie" used for natural history education by the University of Minnesota's Landscape Arboretum, in Chanhassen. No matter what the occasion for visiting Schaefer Prairie, visitors and volunteers leave with a greater sense of what the vast and open prairie must have looked like once, hundreds of years ago. —J.K.

Ancient Rituals

SEA TURTLES NESTING, FLORIDA

In the middle of a quiet night, along a stretch of darkened beach, a turtle four to eight feet long and weighing as much as a thousand pounds finally lumbers ashore. Onlookers may have been watching and waiting for hours, drinking coffee to stay awake, and being careful to make as little noise as possible.

Suddenly, there it is: a threatened loggerhead sea turtle (*Caretta caretta*), making its slow and awkward trek to shore, the same way its ancestors did two hundred million years ago.

At such a time, any movement or light can spook the turtle, in which case it will not nest. But if there's no disturbance, she will most likely lay her shelled eggs. It is an intimate moment, and most people simply watch in wonder.

Sea turtles are tough creatures and remain determined to continue their ancient nesting ritual, even on beaches in heavily developed areas. But survival of the various sea turtle species in today's world increasingly depends on our efforts to protect them—along nesting beaches and at sea.

Listed as endangered or threatened by the federal government, all species of sea turtles continue to decline from development, pollution, dredging, and collisions with boats and other human influences. So keeping nesting areas intact—in places such as Florida—is especially important. The state is a nesting haven for about 90 percent of all loggerheads in the hemisphere and 80 percent of all sea turtles in the continental United States.

Each summer, female sea turtles come ashore Florida beaches to lay about one hundred eggs each. They deposit these eggs in nests, cover them with sand, and return to the sea. Two months later, hatchlings emerge as a group from their nest and scurry into the water. Only one in a thousand turtles will survive to adulthood. In the course of its life, it will travel around and across whole oceans by passive drifting or active migration, with an instinctive yet still mysterious sense of direction.

The Nature Conservancy's Blowing Rocks Preserve on Jupiter Island, Florida, is a major nesting sanctuary for loggerheads, as well as for green and leatherback turtles. The preserve's mile-long Atlantic beachfront has immense appeal to the sea turtles, apparently because of the darkness and serenity of Jupiter Island, where homes are set back from the coastal strand. All three of these species come ashore to nest at Blowing Rocks from late March through September.

The local community has actively supported the turtles of Blowing Rocks. In 1968, Jupiter Island residents raised more than $1 million to buy and protect 58 acres of the nature preserve. With additional land contributions from local families, the preserve has grown to 73 acres. Conservancy volunteers help conserve nesting areas, watch for hatchlings stranded along the preserve's rocky shoreline, and make sure visitors don't disturb nesting turtles.

As long as we continue to keep coastal areas like Blowing Rocks quiet and undisturbed, and act responsibly while boating, fishing, or just strolling along our beaches, these magnificent creatures will be able to nest and flourish in the Western Hemisphere. —J.B.

WATCHING—AND HELPING— THE TURTLES OF BLOWING ROCKS

The Hawley Education Center at the Blowing Rocks Preserve offers programs and information on sea turtles, habitat restoration, and the natural phenomena of this barrier island. The Indian River Lagoon, a nationally significant estuary that borders the west side of the preserve, contains juvenile fish and shrimp, as well as more than four thousand plant and animal species.

The preserve's name derives from the way the sea breaks against the beach's shoreline, spraying salt water up to fifty feet high. This happens at high tide when ocean conditions are just right, and it's quite a show.

As for seeing nesting turtles, inquire about the Conservancy's guided turtle walks. And remember, protecting the turtles is everyone's responsibility. Here are some tips for the turtle conscious:

➤ Avoid disturbing a turtle that is crawling to or from the ocean.
➤ Avoid crowding around a sea turtle, and never touch one.
➤ Avoid shining lights in her eyes or snapping flash photos.
➤ Sit quietly in the dark, at a distance, to watch her nest.
➤ Discourage others from disturbing sea turtles.

Endings and Beginnings

ELKHORN SLOUGH, CALIFORNIA

If there is magic on this planet, it is contained in water.
—LOREN EISELEY, *The Immense Journey*

Tucked into the graceful curve of California's Monterey Bay, midway between Monterey and Santa Cruz, Elkhorn Slough flows nearly seven and a half miles inland. The ancient river channel follows the rolling land and spills into a jagged maze of tidal creeks, mudflats, and marshes that cover more than 3,000 acres.

Elkhorn Slough is the second-largest coastal estuary in California. It supports more than 80 species of fish and more than 250 species of birds. The brackish waters teem with life and movement. Tens of thousands of migrating shorebirds depend on the rich lands and waters of the slough for stopover feeding and resting. Many spend the entire winter here—cradled in the safety of the calm waters of the slough, a few miles from the pounding surf of Monterey Bay.

Otters find their way up the winding channel from the bay to hunt the rich waters of the slough and lounge on their backs. Visitors to Elkhorn Slough can stand on shore beneath the great, spreading branches of an oak tree and see shark fins slicing the water. Though it's hard to predict exactly when sharks will swim up the long channel from Monterey Bay, dozens of sharks frequently swarm in the slough's shallow waters at high tide, feeding, breeding, and giving birth to live young.

August at Elkhorn Slough is a time of ends and

beginnings. The long months of sun-drenched summer are almost over, and the waters of the slough are supersalty from evaporation. The estuary is seasonal, with freshwater runoff occurring only in the rainy months. As fall comes on, the mudflats and banks along the slough are covered with blazing yellow flowers of field mustard, blue dicks, lupine, and red-stem filaree. The tangled mats of succulent pickleweed are beginning to turn from pale green to crimson, the signal of changing seasons. Poison-oak leaves show bright shades of yellow, orange, and red, all heralds of the coming changes.

The birds also begin to arrive. Resident and migratory birds nest and chatter among the oaks along the slough. Northern flickers and downy woodpeckers perch in the branches, and hawks and owls build their nests among the thick, swaying branches of the taller trees. Down in the sticky mud along the water's edge, sandpipers, dowitchers, willets, avocets, marbled godwits, and

herons hunt for food, their footprints crossing and recrossing in thin lines that trail off to the shallows. In the wider, open waters coots, pintails, teal, shovelers, and western grebes climb and dive in the air above the slough. Brown pelicans, peregrine falcons, and snowy plovers also find shelter among the lands and waters here.   —C.B.

HISTORY OF ELKHORN SLOUGH PRESERVE

More than five thousand years ago, Costanoan Indians established villages along the shores of Elkhorn Slough. They hunted tule elk and waterbirds and gathered the slough's abundant shellfish. Today, scattered middens and shell mounds indicate the old village sites. In some places, the bones of otters and sea lions have also been found among the remains.

By the late 1800s American settlers had established homes and farms in the surrounding uplands. Fields and orchards dotted the hills and valleys of the Elkhorn area. Grain from nearby farms was shipped down the slough to Moss Landing, where it was loaded onto coastal schooners bound for San Francisco.

When the Southern Pacific Railroad expanded in the 1870s along the edge of the slough, it reduced the need for coastal shipping. Trains still clatter along the tracks a few yards from the preserve. Resource use has changed much over the last two hundred years. Now the area supports dairy farms, livestock, and agricultural operations; a major fishing port; and a marine research facility.

Hawk Highways

CAPE MAY BIRD MIGRATION, NEW JERSEY

At Cape May, time is still told by the annual return of the birds.

Cape May, New Jersey, where the tip of the New Jersey peninsula juts out between the Atlantic Ocean and Delaware Bay, is one of the top birding areas in the world. The combination of land and water attracts hundreds of species of birds each year as they follow the winds and weather of the Atlantic Flyway on their annual fall migration to South America.

In the last days of August, the brackish marshes of the Cape May Migratory Bird Refuge and other nearby preserves begin to fill with the chirps and calls of countless thousands of songbirds. As the bright days of summer fade into the gentle bronze of autumn, large numbers of raptors will also find their way to Cape May. They will dive from the sky to hunt in the shallow wetlands and stop to rest in the thick grassy meadows.

Late-summer visitors to the refuge get an early, leisurely glimpse of the coming flocks. The pace here is slow at this time of the year, and patient observers get to see the first of the hawks swoop in on an updraft.

A trail through the preserve snakes along a mile of undeveloped beachfront. Here, the Atlantic throws itself against the soft sand and rolls back out in an unceasing tide of movement. Earlier in the year, during the spring migration, least terns and piping plovers scurried along the packed sand at the waterline and built their nests in shallow depressions in front of undisturbed beach dunes. Each year, volunteers build careful fences

WINGS OF THE AMERICAS

The birds of the Americas represent nearly half of the world's 9,700 bird species. They also reflect something more: the health of our ecosystems and the rich natural heritage that defines the New World.

Whether migratory or resident, the birds of North America, Latin America, and the Caribbean have one thing in common: loss of habitat is hurting their ability to thrive and, in some cases, to survive.

Urbanization, agricultural use, and other land development in North America continue to fragment forested lands. In Latin America and the Caribbean, economic and agricultural pressures are quickly consuming lands rich in biodiversity and crucial to the survival of both native and migratory birds.

The Nature Conservancy's Wings of the Americas program, made possible by Canon U.S.A., Inc., seeks to address this problem by taking a long-term, comprehensive approach to conserving key lands that support birds at risk throughout our hemisphere. The program gathers information and takes action; connects birds, people, and habitats for comprehensive conservation; and does on-the-ground conservation.

Birds such as royal terns, common terns, and killdeers that stop each year to rest among the lands and waters of the Cape May Migratory Bird Refuge eventually find their way down ancient flyways to the rich but threatened habitats of Latin America. Wings of the Americas has the unique ability to link and coordinate conservation efforts to protect our birds of the Americas at their breeding grounds, stopover sites, and wintering areas.

For more information about Wings of the Americas, visit the Conservancy's Web site.

around the nests to mark them and protect them from damage.

But at Cape May the fall migration is time for the raptors, the majestic birds of prey. Dedicated birders come to fill their life lists with sightings of Cooper's hawks, ospreys, sharp-shinned hawks, and peregrine falcons. Before the harsh winds of winter blow from the ocean, eighty thousand birds of prey will stop among the marshes and meadows to rest and prepare for the long journey south. Fifteen species of raptors use the entire Cape May peninsula as temporary shelter during the fall migration.

The hawks and the falcons will come to hunt voles and other small game in the grasslands away from the ocean. And a few lucky visitors may see eagles and ospreys hunting for fish in the smooth water of ponds and creeks. The kestrels will darken the sky above the preserve, and even the bright wings of monarch butterflies and the iridescent bodies of dragonflies will light the low grasses along the wetlands.   —C.B.

The Aesthetics of Cranes

SANDHILL CRANES MIGRATING, NORTH DAKOTA

Our ability to perceive quality in nature begins, as in art, with the pretty.
It expands through successive stages of the beautiful to values as yet uncaptured by language.
The quality of cranes lies, I think, in this higher gamut, as yet beyond the reach of words.

—ALDO LEOPOLD, *A Sand County Almanac*

High summer and the colts gambol about the field. The adults solemnly look on as the youngsters toss back their heads and kick up their heels . . . and flap their wings.

Nicknamed colts because of such frisky displays, young sandhill cranes develop long, powerful legs well before their wings mature. At about a month of age, its legs almost finished growing, a crane can run like the wind. By fall, still some months off, these gangly earthbound youths will be able to harness the wind for flight. And once airborne, cranes are about as graceful in flight as a bird can be.

Squadrons of cranes, precision in chevrons, descend out of the skies onto North American fields and wetlands during their biannual migrations north and south. The fall is a good time to observe cranes in North Dakota, at The Nature Conservancy's Davis Ranch Preserve and John E. Williams Memorial Preserve—especially if you come at the break or end of day. Throughout the Midwest and the plains, aggregations numbering into the hundreds and hundreds of thousands of cranes are not an uncommon sight. Unlike their more solitary cousins, the herons, cranes migrate in large numbers, and a popular marsh during migration can seem nearly shoulder to shoulder in four-foot-tall *Grus canadensis*.

To witness a gathering of the snake-necked cranes today on a mist-shrouded bog is to think

ALDO LEOPOLD

Among the essays collected in Aldo Leopold's 1949 *A Sand County Almanac,* his "Marshland Elegy" ranks as one the most moving. Leopold's essay is both an evolutionary history lesson and a passionate lament for sandhill cranes and the destruction of their habitats by development. Bitterly, Leopold asks, "The high priests of progress knew nothing of cranes, and cared less. What is a species more or less among engineers? What good is an undrained marsh anyhow?"

Leopold, who was born in 1887 and died in 1948, helped define American environmental thought, along with figures such as Henry David Thoreau and John Muir. Leopold was a U.S. Forest Service employee early in his career, which prompted him to become a provocateur for better conservation policies and practices. Later, he taught at the University of Wisconsin, where today the Aldo Leopold Chapter of the Society for Conservation Biology and Aldo Leopold Chair in Restoration Ecology testify to his lasting contributions to environmental science.

Leopold is best known in environmental circles for his essay "The Land Ethic," included in *A Sand County Almanac.* In it, Leopold argues that nonhuman life, or collectively "the land," be given ethical consideration as part of the life "community" of which humans are but one "plain member and citizen." "The Land Ethic," with its emphasis on preserving the "integrity, stability, and beauty of the biotic community," underpins the rationale and direction of much modern conservation work, including that of The Nature Conservancy.

of the probable ancestors of all birds: dinosaurs. Making a series of loud, eerie, guttural calls, croaks, and rattles, cranes seem primordial, a holdover from another time. The sandhill crane itself evolved during the Eocene epoch, thirty-eight million years ago, making it one of the few animals to survive today, while "other members of the fauna in which he originated are long since entombed within the hills," as naturalist Aldo Leopold once observed. An individual crane can live for forty years.

Gatherings of cranes are found in scattered sites throughout North America; during migration cranes favor major flyways through the Great Plains and Great Lakes. The mix of prairie and wetlands at Davis Ranch and the John E. Williams Memorial Preserve couldn't be more ideal habitat for cranes as they migrate through. Over the course of a year, cranes are distributed from the tundra of the Bering Straits to the marshlands of the southeastern United States and Mexico. Some cranes migrate as far as seven thousand miles and can fly at such an altitude as to be too high to be seen from the ground.

Worldwide, there are fourteen species of cranes, some of which are endangered. In North America populations of sandhill cranes, down earlier in the century, have rebounded in recent years because of wildlife refuges and voluntary conservation by private landholders.

A relative, the whooping crane, often shares habitat with the sandhills during migration. The whooping crane (which can let out a loud namesake *whoop!*) is one the most endangered North American birds, driven to near extinction by hunting and habitat loss. Repopulation attempts have met with some success. Like the sandhill, the whooper is a striking sight, wading on long legs at dawn through the bottomlands, at once recalling an ancient past and foretelling a future that, ideally, will always resound with cranes. —J.K.

A U T U M N

Autumn is the changeling season. It tests your heart as sometimes love can. Beginning warm and rich in September, it becomes vivid and expansive in October but by November starts to show its wear, with a taste of Arctic air in December and a dusting of snow. Lament autumn's inevitable fade or embrace it—or, better still, adapt to it, since autumn isn't going to change its ways.

Wild things in the United States have clearly chosen the latter strategy. Through motion and rootedness, they adapt. Hawks in Connecticut, cranes in Kansas, and salmon in Oregon, driven by the season's slide, know instinctively they must *be elsewhere, while in contrast, an aspen grove in Nevada—each tree connected to the others through underground rhizomes—waits out the fall, its leaves trembling. Still other life is hardly shaken by autumn—the tough-skinned alligators of Texas, veterans of countless seasons; resident albino cave creatures in Kentucky; the sea life of tidal pools in Maine and coral reefs in Florida, oblivious to what the weather is doing up top.*

The paradox of autumn, as Emerson notes of nature in general, is its capacity to elicit "wild delight" in us "in spite of real sorrows." The trick, he tells us, is not to be waylaid by the sorrow: "Not the sun or summer alone, but every hour and season yields its tribute of delight."

Good advice.

Pool Creatures

TIDAL POOL, MAINE

*When the tide is high on a rocky shore, when its brimming fullness creeps up
almost to the bayberry and the junipers where they come down from the land, one might
easily suppose that nothing at all lived in or on or under these waters of the sea's edge.*

—RACHEL CARSON, *The Edge of the Sea*

The shallow, clear seawater of the tidal pool acts as magnifier. The blood-red common starfish that looks palm-sized is actually barely larger than a silver dollar; scuttling crabs are only as big as a thumbnail; tortoiseshell limpets measure maybe an inch across; and individual barnacles and periwinkles are no larger than pencil heads. The demands of the sea—the relentless pounding surf and the powerful tides—do not favor great size among Maine's tidal pools' inhabitants.

In The Nature Conservancy's Rachel Carson Salt Pond Preserve, a quarter-acre tidal pool on the Atlantic amid a 77-acre preserve, life is spent partly in and partly out of water for many of the plants and animals, and they have adapted to such extremes accordingly. With the tide high, barnacles open their shells underwater and stick out a feathery appendage to snag microscopic food from the sea. When the tide recedes to expose phalanxes of these white barnacles to the air, clinging to rocks, the creatures close their shells tight against the elements (the portals resemble the circular shape of a submarine door), awaiting the tide's return.

Other pool creatures, such as blue mussels and a number of species of periwinkles, behave similarly, opening up beneath the water and sealing up tight above. Periwinkles are miniature grazers, feeding on rock algae and weeds, moving forward—as their kind is apt—at a snail's pace. But a large population of peri-

RACHEL CARSON, NATURALIST

Rachel Carson is most famous for her environmental tocsin *Silent Spring*. In fact, some credit her 1962 book that warned of the systemic damage of chemical pesticides, notably DDT, as the start of the modern environmental movement.

Before this, Carson spent her early professional life as a marine biologist with the U.S. Fish and Wildlife Service. Her first three books were about the sea, including *Under the Sea-Wind* (1941), the best-seller *The Sea Around Us* (1951), and *The Edge of the Sea* (1955).

To research *The Edge of the Sea*, Carson visited the very Nature Conservancy tidal pool that would one day bear her name, as well as others up and down the Maine coast. Carson's involvement with Maine's natural world went even beyond her lyrical, forceful prose and her work as a marine biologist. Carson, who lived in Maine for a period, helped found the Maine chapter of the Conservancy. The Rachel Carson Salt Pond Preserve was dedicated in 1970, as was the Rachel Carson National Wildlife Refuge, near Wells, Maine.

Carson remained modest about the immediate, ground-shaking impact *Silent Spring* had on American environmental policies and actions. Eventually—though Carson would not live to see it, dying in 1964 from a long battle with cancer—*Silent Spring* would lead to bans on many chemicals such as DDT and, indirectly, the passage of legislation recognizing the value of non-human life, such as the Endangered Species Act in 1973.

Carson once wrote to a friend, "The beauty of the living world I was trying to save has always been uppermost in my mind—that, and anger at the senseless, brutish things that were being done. . . . Now I can believe I have at least helped a little."

winkles moving slowly for centuries is a formidable force, eventually scraping away rock surfaces, grain by grain, and deepening the tide pool.

Another marine snail, the dog whelk, uses its radula not to scrape rocks, as periwinkles do, but to bore into its hard-shelled prey, which includes mussels and periwinkles. To get at barnacles, the dog whelk either uses this technique or pries a barnacle's portal open to get at the soft creature within. As with much at the tidal pool, the slow speed and small scale at which this carnivorous drama plays itself out escapes the human eye.

The plants that live at the tidal pool also vary their behavior in and out of the sea. Brown rockweed at low tide lays supine at the water's edge, wilted and seemingly dead. But when the tide returns, it resurrects itself, standing tall underwater, floating on small air bladders. At high tide, rockweed, kelp, sea colander, knotted wrack, sea lettuce, Irish moss, and other plants turn the tidal pool into an underwater forest.

Perhaps the strangest denizens of this tidal pool are creatures that look like plants but are actually animals. The clava, for example, looks like an underwater flower, pink-tinged and petaled. Swaying in the underwater currents, the clava's tentacles are tipped with poison cells that can paralyze a worm, small crustacean, or other sea creature. And with these same flowery tentacles, the clava seizes and transports the victim downward into its maw.

The great naturalist Rachel Carson, who studied these creatures and in honor of whom this tidal pool is named, is quite right that at high tide the salt pond looks to be like any other stretch of rugged Maine coast. But as Carson observed and wrote about so eloquently, as the tide ebbs, the pool's beauty, wonderment, and struggles between life and death reveal themselves—briefly, until the waters come again.—J.K.

Swamped!

BOREAL BOG, WEST VIRGINIA

Hope and the future for me are not in the lawns and cultivated fields,
not in towns and cities, but in the impervious and quaking swamps.

—HENRY DAVID THOREAU

As dawn stretches its long arms over a cloudless early-September sky, a fly makes the fatal decision to stop on a boreal swamp's insectivorous sundew plant. Within seconds, the dew-like drops of sticky fluid exuded by the sundew's glandular leaf hairs entrap the unsuspecting insect. Nearby, a light wind bobs the fuzzy white heads of a cotton-grass field as if to laugh at the fly's misfortune. A closed huddle of showy purple blooms stands ignorant in the moist peat bog.

The Nature Conservancy's Cranesville Swamp Preserve is a classic example of a northern boreal swamp community, and features boreal species more typical of central Canada than its location in West Virginia, miles below the Mason-Dixon line. Here, nestled within the Allegheny Plateau of northeastern West Virginia and western Maryland, a unique cradle of northern plants flourishes in this relict community tucked away since the last ice age.

Over fifteen thousand years ago, a great ice sheet advanced over the northern United States and Canada, pushing northern species south. Although the ice itself never reached West Virginia or Maryland, it created a colder climate, and the northern species thrived. Eventually, the earth's climate warmed and the ice and northern species retreated north again. However, in a few places, like Cranesville Swamp, a special combination of natural circumstances allowed northern species to remain and survive.

At an elevation of 2,500 feet, the swamp is a microclimate, remaining cooler than the surrounding lowlands throughout the year. In the spring and fall, cold night air flows down the swamp's surrounding hills, displacing the warmer air on the swamp floor. This inversion creates frost pockets, often causing the swamp's trees to turn autumn colors well before those on higher ground. Thus, the cold climate and enduring

THE MURKY WETLAND STORY

AN OVERVIEW OF WETLAND TYPES

From Florida's mangrove forests to Alaska's coastal marshes, wetland habitats occur where the water table is at or near the surface long enough to support water-loving soils and plants. Varying in shape, size, type, and function, wetlands provide flood and erosion control, water-quality maintenance, and support to a wide variety of life.

➤ Bogs: Partially decomposed remains of plants and animals make up a bog's characteristic organic soils, known as peat. Lacking good drainage, bogs are found in cooler regions, where temperatures and limited oxygen in the water discourage organic material breakdown.

➤ Fens: A fen's highly productive habitat is largely influenced by groundwater, such as flowing streams, creating a steady nutrient supply. Fens are wet year-round and have good drainage.

➤ Marshes: Usually well drained, these treeless areas remain wet year-round. Freshwater marshes, making up nearly 90 percent of our nation's wetlands, are found along the shallow edges of ponds, lakes, rivers, and streams; they have a high year-round water table. Coastal marshes flood daily with ocean water at high tides.

➤ Swamps: These forested wetlands are usually poorly drained areas on the edges of lakes and streams.

➤ Vernal Pools: Small, isolated wetlands characterized by flooding in the winter and spring and drying in the summer and fall, these pools are vital to amphibian breeding and survival.

moisture offer the same environment as that of northern United States and Canadian bogs.

The swamp's nutrient-poor and acidic soils, called peat, are dominated by mats of sphagnum and peat mosses. Lacking good drainage, the swamp collects partially decomposed plant debris, which is compacted into peat, making the swamp a peatland bog. Representing various stages of bog and forest succession, nineteen different plant communities, ranging from shrubby wetlands to hardwood forests, occur here. Specially adapted wildflowers, such as the creeping snowberry, goldthread, and marsh marigold, don't mind the swamp's difficult environment and year-round wetness. Some species have adapted specific traits to survive, such as the northern water shrew's ability to run on water, a talent it uses to escape lurking saw-whet owls.

Most trees are unable to survive in the swamp's harsh conditions. Skirting the perimeter and sprinkled throughout the swamp, hemlock, red spruce, Canada yew, red maple, black cherry, and yellow birch can be found. Tamarack, or American larch (*Larix laricina*), a deciduous member of the pine family, reaches its southern limit here, growing sparsely among the sedges and cranberries. By late September, the tamarack's needles turn bright yellow, making the trees easily distinguishable from their hemlock and spruce relatives. Years ago, early settlers believed that ancient Native Americans cleared this land before the settlers arrived. Now scientists know that the lack of trees is a natural fact of an acidic bog.

Protected since 1960, Cranesville Swamp was one of the first national natural landmarks to be designated by the National Park Service. Visitors can stroll the preserve's boardwalk, stopping for a moment to listen for the golden-crowned kinglet, alder flycatcher, and Nashville warbler, or just to watch the cotton grass bob in the wind. Somewhere in this three-mile-long, quarter-mile-wide northern swamp showcase, another small fly seals his fate and another sundew has breakfast.—L.A.

The Muck of Marshes

CHEYENNE BOTTOMS MIGRATORY BIRDS, KANSAS

Never have I seen such quantities of swans, cranes, pelicans, geese, and ducks as were here. The swamp was fairly covered with them, and they seemed to feel so safe that I could have killed hundreds of them with the shot of my double-barreled weapon.

—DR. FREDERICK WISLIZENUS,
ST. LOUIS PHYSICIAN AND NATURALIST, ON VISITING CHEYENNE BOTTOMS, 1841

Thank goodness for the muck of marshes.

They're certainly not pretty, but the mudflats of Cheyenne Bottoms in Kansas have what it takes to lure whooping cranes making the three-thousand-mile jaunt from northern Canada to the Gulf Coast. Here hungry birds find the tender protein-rich morsels—plant roots and aquatic animals—that are their staff of life. There are fewer than 250 whooping cranes left in the world; we probably wouldn't have them if it weren't for stopovers like the Bottoms.

Covering more than 27,000 acres of south-central Kansas, Cheyenne Bottoms is a key part of the Central Flyway, a migratory route used by thousands of waterfowl and shorebirds each year. There is no larger system of wetlands in the state. Each spring and fall, hundreds of thousands of foraging birds—nearly half of all North American shorebirds migrating east of the Rocky Mountains—litter the Bottoms' larger pools of water, extensive mudflats, and small puddles surrounded by prairie grass.

About 320 species have been spotted here. They include five endangered and threatened species—the whooping crane, bald eagle, peregrine falcon, least tern, and piping plover—and such unusual visitors as the roseate spoonbill, anhinga, and brant. As long as there is water in the marshes, there are birds at the Bottoms. Migrating ducks and cranes reach their peak numbers in late March and early April. Migrating shorebirds begin arriving in late March and reach a critical mass from late April to late May.

According to scientists who have drilled through a hundred feet of marsh sediment, the silt at the bottom of the Bottoms is about one hundred thousand years old. That makes this an ancient foraging ground.

There's a method to the seemingly random foraging. Different birds eat in different ways, preferring habitats of varying water depth, vegetation height, and density. Some forage in dry mud, others in as much as seven inches of water. There are places—from sparsely vegetated mudflats to moderately vegetated open shallow water—to suit every need.

For many birds, the favorite food is the mud-dwelling larvae of midges, also known as bloodworms. At times, there are as many as fifty larvae in each square inch of mud, some over one inch long. Tender morsels, indeed! Entomologists estimate the shorebirds eat about 330,000 pounds of bloodworms each spring.

The Nature Conservancy has protected more than 7,000 acres at Cheyenne Bottoms Preserve since its first land acquisition there, near Grand Bend, in 1990. Much of the work involves restoring and monitoring habitat to ensure the conditions favored by migrating birds. Alien species, such as salt cedar, or tamarisk, have to be removed before they threaten the vitality of the wetland habitat. Areas formerly cropped must be restored to native vegetation. The natural movement of water across the landscape—

known as "sheet flow"—must be preserved by removing old fence rows, roads, and ditches.

Indeed, improved water management is a key to conserving all the wetlands of the Cheyenne Bottoms Preserve, and most Kansas conservation groups are taking part. The stakes are high for one of the world's great migratory bird populations and for Kansas, where the Bottoms have been quite properly called the state's Galápagos, its Amazonia, and its Serengeti—all in one.   —J.B.

WANT TO BUY A DOLLAR'S WORTH OF MUD?

Besides viewing your favorite birds at Cheyenne Bottoms, it's also possible to help protect these marshes. The Kansas chapter of The Nature Conservancy has a Cheyenne Bottoms Adopt-An-Acre Program under which a donation of $300 protects one acre of wetlands at the Bottoms. You can protect lesser amounts—a half acre for $150, a tenth of an acre for $30, even as little as a section twelve feet by twelve feet for $1.

In return for your gift, you'll receive a certificate suitable for framing showing how many acres or feet your gift protected at the Bottoms. With a gift of $50 or more, you'll receive a complimentary one-year gift membership to the Conservancy, and will be mailed the quarterly Kansas newsletter and the bimonthly national magazine.

Visit the Conservancy's Web site for more information.

A Well-Preserved Island

HORN ISLAND, MISSISSIPPI

I left the shore and turned in toward the trees and found, or heard, the most incredible reward.
A symphony of birds . . . the listener was almost overcome by the persistent note of joyous harmony.

—WALTER ANDERSON, *The Horn Island Logs*

There are few deserted, undeveloped islands left these days, but Mississippi's Horn Island is just such a place.

This isolated, windswept island, located approximately eleven miles off the coast of Mississippi, is a study in contrasts to the rapidly developing gulf coastline. Completely undeveloped, Horn Island was formerly a farm and cattle ranch, and is now an officially designated wilderness area and part of the Gulf Islands National Seashore. The island's nearly thirty miles of pristine beachfront, dramatic thirty-foot-high dunes, inland ponds and lagoons, and slash pine forests are all protected by the National Park Service.

Horn Island is a skinny fourteen-mile island, one of four barrier islands that hug the Mississippi coast and protect it from the full force of heavy seas and storms. The island is home to an astounding variety of plants and animals that thrive here despite extreme temperature variations, high humidity, and severe storms.

The Nature Conservancy occasionally sponsors trips to Horn Island, including trips to clean up its beaches. Visitors who arrive by boat first notice the clarity of its clear blue waters, its white quartz beaches, and its warm gulf breezes. Some people visit the island to hike, bird-watch, or beachcomb, while others come here to escape and study nature.

Fall is a particularly good time to visit, when migrating monarch butterflies dot the air and the island becomes a stopover point for neotropical migratory birds, including the ruby-throated and rufous hummingbirds. Weary sanderlings rest here before continuing on their marathon journey from the Arctic to South America. At least four species of flycatchers and four species of sparrows can be found on the island during fall migration, along with many other species.

Horn Island is known for the variety of its birds— over 280 species have been listed here. Endangered and threatened birds spotted at the island include brown pelicans, bald eagles, peregrine falcons, piping plovers, least terns, and red-cockaded woodpeckers.

Dolphins swim alongside the boats that anchor on the quieter lee side of the island. Visitors must wade in to the beach, carefully watching where they plant their feet. They are advised to shuffle their feet when wading, to advertise their presence to the local stingray population.

In these shallow waters, more agreeable creatures can also be found: squid, shrimp, silversides, mullet, and horseshoe crabs all live here. On the beach, seashells, sharks' teeth, and other natural treasures often surface after high tide.

Hiking in the narrow interior is difficult due to dense, tangled vegetation, but it provides intrepid explorers a completely different view of the island. Beneath the canopy of slash pine, alligators bask beside brackish ponds and lagoons. A variety of lizards, snakes, and turtles, including the threatened loggerhead sea turtle, can also be found on the island.

The island is also home to a host of small mammals. Nutria, otters, rabbits, rats, and raccoons either washed ashore on flood debris or were introduced by humans. Red wolves were introduced in 1989 as a propagation project and produced several litters of pups. The National Park Service hoped the wolves would be able to control exotic species such as cottontail rabbits and nutria.

This small wilderness island belies the tremendous diversity of life that abounds on its shores.   —A.P.

BARRIER ISLANDS

Mississippi's barrier islands were formed by quartz sand that washed down mountain streams over thousands of years into the Gulf of Mexico. Strong gulf currents pushed the sand out into the shallow sea, until eventually exposed ridges appeared. Even today, wind, tides, and storms are perpetually manipulating the shape, size, and even the very existence of the islands.

Barrier islands take the brunt of storms along the heavily populated Mississippi Gulf Coast. As such, they protect valuable property and extensive coastal marshlands, including the Pascagoula River Watershed, the largest undredged and unchannelized river system in North America. These marshlands are crucial nurseries for the aquatic life that helps maintain biodiversity and also support the economy through commercial and sportfishing.

Trembling Aspen

FALL COLORS, NEVADA

A woodland in full color is awesome as a forest fire, in magnitude at least;
but a single tree is like a dancing tongue to warm the heart.

—HAL BORLAND, *Sundial of Seasons*

Mojave summers fill southern Nevada with light and heat and dust, but 8,000 feet into the sky near Las Vegas, autumn comes early to Kyle Canyon. One steep, narrow road climbs into the canyon through changing vegetation and dropping temperatures. Visitors begin on the desert floor, then ascend through creosote bushes and bur sage, Joshua trees and junipers, until, finally, the road rises and winds among thick stands of pines and oaks and aspens. Hikers who come here in search of the season's color crunch through trails covered with fallen leaves and pine needles to breathe the sharp, clear smells of autumn.

Kyle Canyon, high above the harsh desert, changes with the seasons. In the fall, the shadows deepen among the limestone cliffs. Giant ponderosa pines spice the air with the crisp scent of pine tar, already a hint of the upcoming winter. Thickets of Gambel oaks shake off their summer green and burst with autumn color. These are the red and orange leaves that midwesterners recognize from childhood autumns in Illinois and Missouri and Ohio.

The aspens are here, too. Through the spring and summer, the round green leaves tremble on slim branches and glow silver in the light. In the quiet of Kyle Canyon, it sometimes seems the leaves jingle in the wind. The tree is named for the poetry of its movement: *Populus tremuloides*, trembling aspen. In autumn, the small, round aspen leaves shimmer and turn golden in the clear air. Aspens rise from the sides of the canyons, tucked in gullies and avalanche chutes, blazing from the land—each tree seems tipped with fire.

Rusty copper-colored leaves fall across the trails, and pines and the white firs lift green canopies into the deep blue skies. Clark's nutcrackers dance from branch to branch in the cool, bright air of this sky island. Their chatters and calls are the only clear sounds heard above the wind. Among these trees and higher in the bristlecone pines of upper Kyle Canyon, a suite of more than thirty unique plants, butterflies, and one mammal—a chipmunk—reside with the raucous nutcrackers.

Fall visitors to Kyle Canyon can begin to feel the ground hardening beneath their feet. They can hear the quiet of winter coming through the gentle winds that stir the dry leaves. Bare branches stretch dark and mysterious against the sky, and fall is like silver in the air here. Hikers dig their fingers into the layers of fallen leaves and pine needles. The sharp, brittle oak leaves crumble in their hands and smell like smoke. The red and golden aspen leaves scatter along the trails like ticker tape to usher in another autumn.   —C.B.

WHY LEAVES CHANGE COLOR

The brilliant reds and yellows of autumn leaves are also there throughout the spring and summer—they just can't be seen. All leaves contain yellow and orange carotenoids, but during most of the year, these "fall" colors are masked by the green of chlorophyll.

Leaves produce a tree's food and nutrients. Chlorophyll absorbs energy from the sun and uses it to change carbon dioxide and water into carbohydrates, sugars, and starches that serve as the tree's food. During the spring and summer, this continues nonstop. But in the fall, shorter days and falling temperatures cause this process to slowly end.

When the leaf stops producing food, the chlorophyll starts to break down, and other colors within the leaf become visible. Sometimes other chemical changes take place within a leaf and give rise to additional color shades ranging from red to yellow to blue. These colors create the reddish purples, deep oranges, and dazzling yellows of dogwoods, sugar maples, and aspens.

The weather affects the brilliance of all colors. The best conditions for bright, colorful leaves are warm, sunny days and cool nights.

Old Man of the Marsh

ALLIGATOR VIEWING, TEXAS

As the sun sets, a brackish marsh near Matagorda Bay on Texas's Gulf Coast comes alive. A flock of birds lands to feed briefly in the shallow water, swinging their heads from side to side. Grebes and coots swim past a great egret's long legs, while a belted kingfisher calls from a low bush. Two round alligator eyes watch the commotion from the waterline—motionless, waiting.

American alligators (*Alligator mississippiensis*) have survived almost unchanged since the days of the dinosaurs. Once common in coastal areas, this amazing and often misunderstood resident of the southeastern United States was at one time hunted to near extinction.

Today, protected by federal laws, alligator populations have begun to recover, from the Carolinas down to Florida and over to Texas.

During fall, winter, and early-spring days at The Nature Conservancy's Clive Runnells Family Mad Island Marsh Preserve, visitors can often see alligators sunning throughout the preserve's intertidal and freshwater wetlands.

For many of the marsh's inhabitants, the alligators' activities are important for survival. During the dry winter season, alligators sweep their powerful tails to create deep "gator holes" in the soft soil. The large holes can hold water throughout a drought, providing a needed foraging area for many resident species, such as wading birds. Alligators also help marsh ecology by creating walking paths in the grass. These matted areas often widen to form creeks during the rainy season, helping to flood the marsh.

In the wild, an adult alligator lives for thirty-five to fifty years, reaching close to thirteen feet in length and six hundred pounds. Although alligators are often confused with crocodiles, an alligator's snout is short, blunt, and rounded, as compared to the crocodile's long, tapered snout. Alligators are extremely agile and quick, capable of fast bursts of speed for short distances. Some say an alligator can outrun a horse for a distance of thirty feet.

Feeding primarily at night, alligators eat fish, turtles, small mammals, snakes, birds, and even smaller alligators. This tough diet quickly wears down an alligator's eighty teeth, though they do grow back over time. In a lifetime, a single alligator can go through two to three thousand teeth. Early humans believed alligator teeth to have a magical power to ward off snakebites, since alligators appeared to be immune to snake venom. This myth was later explained by the alligator's protective "armor," the extremely tough skin and bony back plates that prevent snake fangs from penetrating the hide.

Once an alligator reaches about four feet, its only real predator is man. For an alligator, sexual maturity depends more on the size of the animal—a length of about six feet—than its age. During late March and April, complex courtship rituals involving touching, rubbing, bubble blowing, and vocalizations can be seen and heard throughout the marsh. Mating takes place in open water. Then the female returns to the shoreline to construct a mounded nest of plants and mud. Laying approximately forty eggs, the alligator mother protects her nest until the babies hatch, sixty-five days later. The sex of the young is determined by the eggs' incubation temperature, which ranges from 86 to 93 degrees Fahrenheit. The eggs in the intermediate temperature range (90.5 to 91.4 degrees) produce exclusively males, though a smaller percentage of males are produced at temperatures as low as 88.7 and as high as 92.8 degrees. Females are produced as the incubation temperature moves higher or lower from the intermediate-range temperature.

Today alligators thrive at Mad Island Marsh Preserve, but that wasn't always the case. Once a premier freshwater ecosystem, the marsh's abundant and diverse wildlife population began to disappear during the 1980s as the delicate balance between salt water and fresh water started to change. Now conservation protects this important habitat for sandhill cranes, peregrine falcons, river otters, and bobcats, as well as the alligator.

"Alligators should be respected, not feared," says the Mad Island Marsh Preserve manager, Mark Dumesnil. "You are welcome to canoe through the preserve for a bird's-eye view. Of course, I keep a safe distance between myself and my sunbathing friends."

No thanks. See ya later, alligator.   —L.A.

GATOR OR CROC?

Both members of the Crocodilidae family, alligators and crocodiles are often confused. Adult American alligators are grayish black, reaching an average length of thirteen feet, while American crocodiles tend to be light tan to brownish, reaching an average length of ten to twelve feet. In a crocodile's long and tapered snout, the upper and lower teeth are more or less in line, with the enlarged fourth lower tooth fitting into a notch on the side of the upper jaw. The enlarged teeth are clearly visible outside a closed jaw. In an alligator's short, blunt, and rounded snout, the upper teeth fit outside the lower teeth, with the enlarged fourth tooth fitting into a pit in the upper jaw, thus leaving the enlarged teeth invisible within a closed jaw.

Rarely found in salt water, American alligators inhabit fresh to brackish water in swamps, marshes, lakes, and rivers throughout the southeastern United States, from the Carolinas to Texas. Crocodiles, although found around the world, are very rare in the United States. The American crocodile lives only in the Key West and Florida Bay area and uses special salt-extracting glands to survive in salt water for extended periods of time.

Thanks to legal protection, alligators are no longer endangered. However, despite their remarkable comeback, they continue to be listed as threatened because of their similar appearance to the endangered American crocodile.

The Great Journey

SALMON SPAWNING, OREGON

*Many a time have I merely closed my eyes at the end of yet another troublesome day
and soaked my bruised psyche in wild water, rivers remembered and rivers imagined.*

—HARRY MIDDLETON, *Midnight's Rivers*

Thousands of spring chinook salmon gather at the mouth of the Columbia River each spring to begin their long, arduous migration back to the streams and tributaries where they began life three or four years ago. By fall, these fighting fish will spend their last moments of life in the shallow riffles of a gravel-bottomed stream, spawning another generation of salmon that will follow in their path to the sea.

One hundred years ago, as many as ten million salmon made the annual journey up the Columbia to a multitude of spawning grounds. Today, less than 3 percent of this native run survives.

Though many of their spawning grounds are gone now, one spawning destination is the Middle Fork John Day River, a meandering river that originates in the snowfields of Oregon's Blue Mountains. Several hundred spring chinook salmon (*Oncorhynchus tshawytscha*) still successfully fight their way here each year. These salmon have survived conditions that today are very different from what they were only a century ago.

Instead of struggling against the surging spring currents of the Columbia, they now have to find and "climb" the fish ladders of three major hydroelectric dams, and then cross the slow-moving reservoirs that lie behind the dams. After they turn south into the John Day River, they swim in sun-warmed waters of 80 degrees Fahrenheit or more instead of the cold, cottonwood- and willow-shaded streams they once encountered. By the time the few strong survivors reach their birthplace at The Nature Conservancy's preserve on the Middle Fork, they've navigated 484 miles of obstacles and altered habitats.

Today's annual return, though meager by historic standards, gives conservationists hope. Even before humans entered the picture, only a small fraction of the salmon that hatched ever made it past predators and other hazards all the way to the sea. Fewer still met the tests of survival in the open ocean. And only a remnant—the strongest of the strong—ever arrived home to complete the cycle of life. That is nature's way with salmon.

Despite decades of change from farming, ranching, road building, and logging, the Middle Fork John Day River remains a venerable river of promise. Under the watchful eyes of The Nature Conservancy and its many partners, miles of river near its headwaters are beginning to show signs of recovery. Native willows and sedges are once again growing along the banks, capturing the sediments that will gradually rebuild the stream channel. Former meanders are once again coursing with seasonal floods.

The chinook salmon returning to the Middle Fork are lucky in another way. Many rivers have hosted salmon hatcheries along their banks to replenish stocks for fishing. These hatchery fish are weaker than their wild counterparts and inevitably weaken the native fish runs when they interbreed. Luckily, the John Day River and its tributaries have never had hatcheries along their banks, so the wild fish that spawn here still carry the genetic code of millions of years of evolution.

With redoubled conservation and habitat-restoration efforts, the chinook population can recover, and these wild, pure runs of salmon can continue up the Columbia for centuries to come. —F.A.

RIVERS OF LIFE

Rivers and other fresh waters such as creeks, streams, and lakes shape our lives. Fresh waters provide everything from a rejuvenating drink to biomedical breakthroughs.

A study by The Nature Conservancy has revealed that we *can* make a difference in saving our rivers—if we act quickly.

The study, titled "Rivers of Life: Critical Watersheds for Protecting Freshwater Biodiversity," warns that continued degradation of our nation's rivers and streams could extinguish nearly:

> ➤ 40 percent of U.S. freshwater fish and amphibian species;

> ➤ 66 percent of U.S. mussel species; and

> ➤ 50 percent of U.S. crayfish species.

Freshwater degradation can also harm our drinking water and ultimately damage human health.

But it is not too late. According to the study, if we can protect and restore *as little as 15 percent* of the nation's small watersheds, we can conserve current populations of our freshwater fish and mussel species. Protecting freshwater species will also benefit water quality, human health, and the quality of life in these areas.

On a Wing and an Updraft

HAWK MIGRATION, CONNECTICUT

If it's November, those must be red-tails.

The timing of hawk migrations in various parts of the country tends to be consistent, although extremes in weather and other natural vagaries can delay or even accelerate migration by several weeks. This is to say that particular species of migrating hawks pass through a particular location at about the same time, year after year. So for hawk watchers, September can mean mostly broad-winged hawks. October, American kestrels. November, goshawks.

By November, at The Nature Conservancy's Devil's Den Preserve in western Connecticut, the migration of raptors (hawks, falcons, vultures, and eagles) tends to be dominated by the accipiters, woodland hawks that prey on small birds and animals. Among these are the goshawks, Cooper's hawks, and sharp-shinned hawks. Two species of buteos, larger, stockier hawks, are also present: red-tailed and red-shouldered hawks.

The Den is a particularly good place for hawks and hawk watchers because of its rugged topography. Ridges, outcroppings, ledges, and cliffs form updrafts that hawks use to soar. For hawk watchers poised on these ridges, this means fairly close-in viewing of both individuals and congregations of hawks passing through.

One of the most dramatic sights during hawk migration occurs at Devil's Den and involves large numbers of broad-winged hawks "kettling up." This species of hawk breeds in North America, including at the Den, and migrates to Central and South America for the winter. In the fall, as broad-wings make their way south, they gather into flocks that sometimes number in the thousands. They soar on thermals—warm upward-rising air currents. To use the thermals, the hawks circle, rising ever higher, forming what looks like from the ground a huge kettle in the sky. Once they reach their desired elevation, they pull out of the kettle and soar in a straight path, falling slightly until they reach another thermal and kettle up again.

On a good day at Devil's Den in September, broad-winged hawks kettle up, and visitors can see a couple of hundred spiraling upward. On another good day, during the height of migration in October, hawks passing by a ridge lookout average a bird every ten minutes. Peregrine falcons also pass by, as well as merlins and the occasional northern harrier and osprey. In all, fourteen species of hawks pass through western Connecticut in the fall, with seven species breeding at or near the preserve.

—J.K.

MIGRATION FACTS

➤ At Cape May, New Jersey, up to twelve million birds will fly over during one night.

➤ In the fall the red knot, a shorebird, flies from Baffin Island in the Arctic to Tierra del Fuego at the tip of South America, a trip of eight thousand miles. Then the red knot flies back in the spring. The Swainson's hawk logs between eleven and seventeen thousand migration air miles.

➤ Migrating birds fly most frequently at an altitude roughly between 1,500 and 2,500 feet. A flock of whooper swans were once observed flying at an altitude of more than 28,000 feet—a height favored by jet planes.

➤ Birds migrate by day and night. Generally, passerines (songbirds, by and large) travel by night and birds of prey by day. The passerines travel by night, in part, to avoid birds of prey during the day.

➤ The main wintering grounds for North American birds is Mexico and Central America. Nowhere else is there such an extraordinary concentration of wintering birds—underscoring the importance of habitat preservation in these places.

Fiery Plains

PRESCRIBED BURNS, OKLAHOMA

In Oklahoma, around Nature Conservancy preserves, the smell of fall is sometimes the smell of smoke. And that's good. Autumn is one of the times of the year that the Conservancy uses prescribed burns as way to conserve and manage its nature preserves.

To suggest the use of fire as a conservation tool might seem counterintuitive. For some ecosystems, this would be true. Setting fires in a redwood forest is a bad idea. But in Oklahoma, the vast majority of the region's natural communities depend upon fire to maintain native biological diversity and to keep the landscape as it should be: relatively free of trees.

Grasslands dominate western Oklahoma. Hundreds of prairie plants and insects, dozens of birds, and a suite of small mammals, reptiles, and amphibians are all dependent upon the periodic natural disturbance of fire and what it leaves in its aftermath. Without fire, an invasion of woody species, trees and shrubs, slowly takes place, changing the prairies and open oak savannas into a landscape that might look native, but isn't

truly native. It's also not conducive to the plants and animals of the plains, and nutrients that would be cycled into the soil following a fire are instead lost.

"Native," in ecological terms, simply means particular to that ecosystem. American bison are native to the prairie, for example. Therein lies part of the problem in recent decades with keeping prairies *prairies* in Oklahoma and throughout the Great Plains. Prior to being nearly driven to extinction in the last century, bison were a natural disturbance on the prairie, like wildfires. Their steady grazing prevented woody plants from gaining much of a toehold in the grasslands.

Along with the virtual disappearance of the bison at the end of the last century, settlers also began to suppress wildfires, which had historically been started naturally by lightning. These fires, along with the bison, helped keep the prairie ecosystem in balance and functioning. Additionally, the prairie did get a hand from some humans. Prior to European settlers, historical evidence suggests that Native Americans, for

PRESCRIBED BURNS

The Nature Conservancy's Fire Management and Research Program has been training staff members and restoring fire-dependent landscapes since 1985. The program is rigorous, and Conservancy graduates return to their home states or countries with more than a healthy respect for the inherent dangers of working with such a powerful force.

The specifications for when a prescribed burn can take place on a particular preserve are tight and have as much to do with filling out the paperwork to get legal permission from numerous stakeholders, such as adjacent landowners and township fire departments, as they do with wielding a drip torch properly. Weather conditions, too, must be optimal. This includes the right kind of wind direction and speed, fuel load, moisture content, humidity, and temperatures.

In a prescribed burn, the burn crew utilizes a natural firebreak, if one is available, such as a creek. The crew sets a downwind backfire that creates a "blackline" at which the headfires, set in successive ignitions, will stop. Crew members patrol a "handline" to ensure the burn is contained. Sound complicated? It is. However, Conservancy ecologists, botanists, and biologists are finding that it works—many of the Conservancy's fire-dependent natural communities and their species are thriving with a little fire.

some half a million years, supplemented nature's fires with their own, using prescribed burns to stimulate the growth of food plants, improve forage for game, drive bison, and increase berry crops. Without periodic fires, to use one example, the now imperiled prairie chicken has suffered, since this species requires a patch mosaic of sparse and dense vegetation for its courtship rituals and nesting. Without both habitats, the birds' reproduction success declines.

Of course, today, given the heavy human population in the Great Plains, wildfires could have significant economic and cultural impacts and are not a practical solution to maintaining the prairies' natural state. But prescribed burns are. The Conservancy uses this restoration tool on a number of preserves in Oklahoma and in doing so follows a strict regimen of fire safety so that no private property is damaged. Conservancy staff members are rigorously trained at a prescribed-burn school and must be licensed to burn. They conduct burns only during specific weather conditions.

At Pontotoc Ridge Preserve and Bochler Seeps and Sandhills Preserve, prescribed burns have yielded splendid results. At Bochler, bluejack oak communities that include the rare dwarf pipewort have responded well to periodic prescribed burns that mimic the natural fires that were once a constant feature of the hot summers and dry falls of the state.

One of the Conservancy's landmark preserves, the Tallgrass Prairie, now undergoes a regular cycle of prescribed burns, replicating what scientists believe to have been large fires set by Native Americans each autumn in previous centuries. The Conservancy staff also burns portions of the preserve during the spring and summer to mimic historical seasonal fires and to create a patchwork of prairie vegetation at various stages of growth and renewal.

Further, a large herd of bison are loosed at Tallgrass and allowed to do their part in keeping a remnant of Oklahoma's vast grasslands as it should be—wild and open. —J.K.

The Thin Blue Lines

RIVER LIFE, NEW MEXICO

I effuse my flesh in eddies, and drift it in lacy jags.
—WALT WHITMAN, *Leaves of Grass*

In November, it is still griddle-hot beyond the cottonwoods, but it is cool along the river's edge, with the willows whispering in the wind.

If viewed from the sky, the Gila and Mimbres Rivers of southwestern New Mexico cut through the thirsty brown landscape as thin blue lines—or green lines where the cottonwood forests overhang and obscure the rivers, or yellow lines when the cottonwoods change color in the autumn. No matter what their color, these rivers, largely free-flowing, wild, and clean, are rarities in the American West, where dams and diversions have sapped many a mighty river of its life. The Colorado River, for example, is so impeded along its course that it now seldom completes its southward journey to the sea, but dries up somewhere in Mexico.

Water has defined the modern American West. Well before there were settlers and ranches, and metropolises carved out of the desert, there were flowing rivers and wildlife dependent upon them. The Gila and Mimbres give you a look of what that life was—and still can be, with conservation.

Since 1981 The Nature Conservancy has worked in the Gila River Watershed, an immense area of more than three thousand square miles. The Gila River begins at 11,000 feet at the river's headwaters in the Mogollon, Black, and Pinos Altos Mountains. The Conservancy's Gila Riparian Preserve is miles downstream and protects a classic example of the river. Towering cottonwoods, walnuts, sycamores, alders, and willows make up the riparian, or riverside, forest here. These

THE NATURE CONSERVANCY'S
FRESHWATER INITIATIVE

Who hears the rippling of rivers will not utterly despair of anything.—Henry David Thoreau

Mighty, rolling, and free-flowing, rivers have always drawn us. We build civilizations on their banks. We travel their arteries. We drink their waters and irrigate our fields with their flow. We take fish from them, for food and sport, just as we take pleasure from swimming and boating in them.

And just as rivers give life, so they brim with life.

The United States is a global center of freshwater biodiversity, including 10 percent of all known fish species and almost one-third of all known freshwater mussel species. This diversity is comparable to the terrestrial diversity of the world's great tropical rain forests.

Yet this natural wealth faces serious threats. From California to Maine, and Canada to Chile, fresh waters are dammed, smothered with soil erosion, and lined with development. Already, the United States has lost more than half of its wetlands and riverside ecosystems, and their fish, shellfish, amphibians, and vegetation are following.

Now The Nature Conservancy is joining the cause for rivers. It launched its Freshwater Initiative in 1998 to dramatically increase freshwater conservation in the United States, Latin America, and the Caribbean. The initiative will assist local community groups, natural resource agencies, and other conservation groups involved in land and water management at more than thirty initial sites, ranging from the Altamaha River in Georgia to Madre de las Aguas—"Mother of the Waters"—in the Dominican Republic.

For more information about the Freshwater Initiative program, visit its Web site at www.freshwaters.org.

forests serve double duty as the ecological linchpin in the ecosystem, with their branches providing habitat to many unique and rare birds, such as the Gila woodpecker, southwestern willow flycatcher, black-hawk, and a host of neotropical migrants. The trees' roots stabilize the soil, preventing erosion, which in turn helps water quality, needed by the endangered loach minnow and spikedace.

Today, the forest never strays too far from the riverbank, though in years past more vegetation grew here. Similarly, the marshes and meadows that formed alongside the river's course are largely gone today. The reason behind both phenomena is that the natural flow and ecology of the river have been altered by people. Decades of livestock grazing alongside the river compacted the soil and prevented regeneration. Grazing and fire suppression changed the character of upland soils and vegetation, and the land lost some of its capacity to absorb rainwater. Thus, when hard rains came and flash floods followed, the torrents ripped down through the river channel, scouring away bankside vegetation and soil. Beaver trapping has also contributed to the problem. Beaver dams stem the river's harsh flow and divert water out into the floodplain to create wetlands. Without beaver dams, fewer wetlands exist.

Today, however, the riparian forests of the Gila River and the nearby Mimbres River are regenerating themselves through hands-on restoration, such as keeping grazing animals a good distance away from the rivers and planting saplings along the banks. Other conservation measures as well, including restoring proper flow, promise to bring the rivers back to their former glory beneath the cooling cottonwoods. —J.K.

Working for Nature

RIPARIAN RESTORATION, WYOMING

*Our long-term success depends on unleashing the enormous
latent power of a community's love of place.*

—JOHN C. SAWHILL

Every summer, small parties of volunteers trek through the rugged lands of Wyoming's Big Horn Mountains to pull weeds, catch beetles, and gather seeds at Canyon Creek in the heart of The Nature Conservancy's Tensleep Preserve.

High above the sharp sagebrush plains of the Big Horn Basin, the cold, clear waters of Canyon Creek are a blessing in the harshness of the jagged Wyoming badlands. Here, cooling air drops thundering summer showers on blue and gold meadows of lupine and forests of ponderosa pine.

Mountain lions still roam these sandstone canyons. Ancient petroglyphs and paintings adorn the thick rock walls of box canyons with images of bison and bighorn sheep. The lands are also rich in trembling aspens, cottonwoods, and Douglas firs. The air is warm and soft with the sounds of gentle winds jingling the aspen leaves, and bright rocks shine from the bottom of Canyon Creek.

Volunteers come here every year to help restore the delicate natural balance along the creek bed. Foreign plants have invaded the grassy, shaded borders of Canyon Creek. Without constant monitoring and removal, plants with names like Canada thistle, hound's-tongue, and burdock will crowd out native species and slowly strangle the stream. Volunteers

WYOMING PRESERVES RECREATION PROJECT

Through cooperative and voluntary agreements with owners and managers of public and private lands, The Nature Conservancy has protected nearly 340,000 acres of native Wyoming habitat. These include three Conservancy preserves that are open to the public for low-impact outdoor recreation, natural history study, and stewardship activities.

The Conservancy has joined with the nonprofit National Outdoor Leadership School (NOLS) to design and implement a sustainable recreation-planning and public-education process. Education and outreach efforts related to preserve use will be based on the principles of Leave No Trace, a program dedicated to promoting skills and ethics that enable visitors to enjoy wildlands without harming them. Under Leave No Trace recreation, visitors to natural areas are taught to be aware of fragile environments and to avoid even the smallest action that might upset the delicate ecological balance.

Leave No Trace has six principles:

1. Plan ahead and prepare.

2. Travel and camp on durable surfaces.

3. Pack it in, pack it out.

4. Properly dispose of what you can't pack out.

5. Leave what you find.

6. Minimize use and impact of fire.

creep beneath box elders and willows and lay tape lines through riverside thickets to map out the areas of plants set for removal. The burdock weed, with its sharp smell and hook-and-latch seed ball, is especially tenacious and clings to the land as volunteers with gloved hands tug it out by the roots.

The volunteers are making room for the native species to return along Canyon Creek. The banks will be full of coneflowers, wild roses, blue wild rye, and sweet cicely nodding in the summer breezes. When they have removed the weeds, the volunteers will gather seeds from native plants to aid in restoring the areas they have just cleared. Biologists also gauge the health of the stream by monitoring its beetles, because their numbers and variety are one measure of the diversity of the forest and its stream.

In the afternoon, volunteers stalk the thickets and meadows along Canyon Creek and gather beetles in the soft mesh of butterfly nets. Others peer beneath overturned logs, poking carefully through layers of dead leaves and sand. And still others pry into the furrows of cottonwood bark, searching for beetles. Some are purple and green and iridescent as a peacock feather— they have names like rove beetle, flower beetle, soldier beetle, and hister beetle. From the cold, shallow waters of Canyon Creek a volunteer pulls specimens of stonefly larvae from the gravel wash.

At the end of the day, the volunteers return to camp along trails that wind up into the clear Wyoming sky. They lay their sleeping bags under a clear wash of stars and listen to the strange, low pings of spotted bats circling in the darkness above them.   —C.B.

Under the Sea

The grouper puffed out his cheeks, stuck out his lower lip and made a disagreeable face. . . .
Then his armor-plated head advanced toward me with an unmistakable expression of curiosity.

—JACQUES-YVES COUSTEAU

Crenellated fire, staghorn coral, elkhorn coral, lettuce coral, cactus coral, boulder star coral, sea fan, sea feather, knobby candelabrum, large grooved brain coral, sharp-hilled brain coral, depressed brain coral, and deadman's fingers . . .

The fancifulness of the names of corals is eclipsed only by the appearance of the creatures themselves. Elkhorn *looks* like the horns of an elk. All the brain corals look—unnervingly so— like a human brain. And deadman's fingers can give you a momentary start underwater: did another diver meet an untimely end and is now sealed up in the reef?

Despite the name of this last coral, coral reefs are alive, and what's more, they are predaceous. They are animals that look anything but animal-like and instead appear to be plants or rock. But the live coral use tentacles and other means to snag microscopic plankton. Other forms of sea life are dependent upon coral, attaching themselves to it, nesting in it, hiding in it from predators, using it as hunting grounds, or feeding on it. Together, a coral reef and its dependent marine plants and animals form one of nature's most complex and fascinating symbiotic relationships.

Polyps are the builders of coral reefs. These tiny creatures secrete a hard, limy material that builds the reef. Algae on the reef attract fish by the thousands. One of the more colorful of these is the parrot fish. Schools of parrot fish with their beak-like lips graze on the algae, moving about in a deliberate fashion not unlike

RESCUE THE REEF

Coral reefs, the "rain forests of the ocean," are beautiful and important ecosystems that protect a wide diversity of species. Unfortunately, these reefs are being destroyed by pollution, overfishing, anchor damage, and destructive fishing practices like dynamiting and toxic chemical use. Fish populations are declining and coral growth is slowing. To protect and preserve the coral reefs, The Nature Conservancy established its Rescue the Reef program.

The program's protection efforts focus on practical measures, including hiring and training marine park rangers, installing mooring buoys, funding critical fish surveys, and implementing community outreach programs that promote conservation awareness and compatible development.

Upon making a donation, contributors receive an honorary deed. This deed does not signify ownership but, rather, the commitment to do something specific and tangible to save the critical and threatened ecosystem. In addition, contributors receive information on the area where the reef is located, news of discoveries of marine plants and animals, and updates on the work being done to protect the area. Several times a year, donors will receive the *Global Currents* newsletter and can read about the results being achieved with their investment.

By joining the efforts of the Rescue the Reef program, you will be making a direct and significant impact on the protection and preservation of coral reefs. Please help us safeguard these spectacular reef ecosystems by participating in the Rescue the Reef program. Visit the Conservancy's Web site for more information.

cows on a field of grass. This food chain illustrates the symbioses of reef life: parrot fish and other herbivorous fish keep algae in balance on the reef; otherwise, the algae would overrun the living coral and smother it. It is a delicate balance. In some places in the Caribbean, overfishing has not only decimated fish populations but caused an explosion of algae on certain reefs, and these reefs are dying.

The Florida Keys has the third-largest reef system in the world—and one of the most heavily visited. Tourism, degraded water quality, and overfishing are taking their toll here and on reefs throughout the Caribbean. Though the reefs are miles offshore, they depend on sea grasses and mangroves near the Keys islands to maintain the clear water the coral need to survive. Onshore development and pollution impact the sea grasses and mangroves. In turn, this affects the coral out at sea.

For now, at least, the diversity of coral remains remarkable, with sixty-three species and subspecies of stony corals and forty-two species of octocorals. More than four hundred types of fish, from tiny sergeant majors to giant barracudas, are found around the reefs, as are sea turtles and a variety of marine mammals.

The Nature Conservancy helped create the Florida Keys National Marine Sanctuary to protect 2,600 square nautical miles. Within this immense area are a number of coral reefs. Scuba diving or snorkeling on the reefs here is a spectacular experience—with the caveat that touching corals or the sea creatures found there or anchoring to a reef is absolutely not allowed. To do so kills them.

To float in the current over the top of a coral reef and to view the myriad of life below—from large, thick-lipped groupers to shimmering schools of butterfly fish, to moonfish floating past and spiny lobsters scuttling along the seafloor with their menacing claws up—is transcendent. This reverie, during which you can almost imagine yourself a sea creature, is broken only by the movement of something large and black swimming slowly around the far side of the reef. Your brain tells you, Shark. And then again: *Shark!*

But it is a nurse shark, benign if left alone, and it silently glides past you as you catch your breath underwater.

—J.K.

Twilight World

Caves are home to many mysterious species that live their lives in the permanent twilight and unending darkness beneath our lands and waters.

The world's largest, most extensive cave system exists in Kentucky. Miles of crisscrossing caves lie beneath the state's limestone plains, carved out by ancient streambeds and still-flowing streams. In places, the streams rise again to the surface in mysterious, bottomless sinkholes that dot the landscape and hint at rivers running silently beneath the earth. At the edge of the Cumberland Plateau, the caves around Horse Lick Creek are some of Kentucky's most important natural sites. A few of the caves were once used to collect saltpeter, though many more are still relatively unexplored.

Cavers explore the underground depths; in many cases, the lamps on their helmets are the only lights to ever penetrate the black silence of the cave. Many of the creatures they encounter, like the eyeless crayfish, are blind by design because sight has no place in such an ocean of darkness. The crayfish is pale and spindly, feeling its way along the cave with slender claws and spidery legs. Less than two inches long, it is probably fifty years old, and yet it is still a juvenile. Some eyeless crayfish live to beyond one hundred and may reproduce only three times in a lifetime.

Time moves differently here in this other world. Outside the cave, time and life move around the sun, counting days and seasons. Here in Kentucky's caves, blind fish and pale, ghostly shrimp exist in a world outside of a common concept of time. Day and night mean nothing to the truest of the cave dwellers, known as the troglodytes. They are a diverse group of specialized worms, snails, crayfish, spiders, cave crickets, beetles, fish, and salamanders. They are so thoroughly adapted to their environment that they can never leave.

There are others, though, who come to the caves for temporary refuge but then must leave to eat. Bats use the caves to rest and to protect their young. As day turns to night, the mouths of the Horse Lick Creek caves swarm with bats beating their wings against the twilight in search of a nightly meal of insects. Gray bats, two inches long, with small, round ears and an eleven-inch wingspan, spill from the caves, their hunting squeaks the first call of the evening. The Virginia big-eared bat, named for its one-and-a-half-inch ears perched incongruously on its four-inch body, is rarer and more secretive than its gray cousin. Both bats are endangered and depend on the caves of Horse Lick Creek for habitat.

The caves of Horse Lick Creek are gateways to a dark and relatively unexplored world. But though they seem somehow disconnected and isolated from the land of light and air, they are an important part of intricate ecosystems.

—C.B.

KENTUCKY BAT FACTS

Since they are mammals, bats are more closely related to primates (monkeys, apes, and humans) than they are to birds. There are fourteen species of bats in Kentucky, and over half of them are listed as rare, threatened, or endangered, including the globally endangered gray bat, Indiana bat, and Virginia big-eared bat. These bats generally prefer cave environments, though not all Kentucky bats are cave dwellers. Female Indiana bats use trees for maternity sites. Other species, such as the red bat and the hoary bat, use the leaves of trees as a day roost and migrate south in the winter instead of hibernating. Eastern pipistrelle bats can often be found hanging from the eaves of porches, and colonies of big brown bats are often found behind shutters, while little brown bats are common attic dwellers.

WINTER

For a moment, don't think of winter as only snow and cold. After all, parts of the United States never experience what Annie Dillard observed in Virginia: "It snowed. It snowed all yesterday and never emptied the sky, although the clouds looked so low and heavy they might drop all at once with a thud."

In Hawai`i, winter's a good time for conservationists to remove invasive weeds from the rain forests. In southeast Arizona, Mexican birds and other avian rarities often appear, inexplicably, at a preserve. The Consumnes River of California's Central Valley teems with migratory birds and resident river otters. Farther north, in Oregon, the same can be said of the creatures of the aromatic old-growth juniper forests. Across the country on Long Island, harbor seals arrive from the north and "haul out" of the water to sun themselves in the weak January sun, in blubbery bliss.

Still, if you prefer your winter with some nip, you can go on an owling expedition in Michigan's Upper Peninsula, or join the Christmas Bird Count in Idaho, or track animals in snowy Indiana woods.

Like other seasons, winter is never all one thing or all another. It can be a hybrid. For proof positive, visit Alabama's Little Cahaba River in midwinter, where, despite occasional snow patches and bitter air, the Alabama croton shrub has already begun to unfurl its pale yellow flowers, in defiance of the season.

Jewel of the Peconic

MASHOMACK IN WINTER, NEW YORK

Winter arrives quietly at The Nature Conservancy's Mashomack Preserve, an area of more than 2,000 acres of tidal creeks, woodlands, and fields, edged in white by ten miles of wildlife-rich coastline, all of it sprawling across the southeastern third of Shelter Island, New York.

Here, after the cold sets in, just ninety miles from New York City, red-tailed hawks soar and meadowlarks dart across Mashomack's fields. The great horned owl lives deep inside its woods, and other woodland inhabitants include the tufted titmouse, red-bellied woodpecker, and blue jay.

A visit to the preserve after a fresh snowfall provides observant trackers with evidence of mammals on the preserve. Deer, fox, and raccoon tracks are commonly sighted, and mink tracks have been reported. A river otter was once spotted enjoying a slide down a snow-covered hill.

However, the most dramatic wintertime activity on the preserve is the arrival of thousands of waterfowl from their northern nesting grounds. The Mashomack Preserve has often been called the "Jewel of the Peconic," because it is so important to the conservation of Atlantic Flyway waterfowl. These winter visitors to Mashomack include a grand assortment of dabblers, mergansers, sea ducks, and geese.

By far, the most numerous dabblers, or puddle ducks, are the American black ducks. Several thousand frequent the preserve's shallow creeks and salt marshes, which offer safety as well as plenty of snails to feed upon. A close relative of the familiar mallard, the black duck is found exclusively in eastern North America. It nests throughout the maritime provinces of Canada and winters along the eastern seaboard as far south as the Carolinas. Hunters call the large adult males "red legs," and their brightly colored legs and yellow bills are so distinctive that they were once believed to be a separate species from the females.

In deeper waters on and around the preserve, mergansers and other diving ducks feast upon mussels and slippersnails, herring and killifish. The fish-eating red-breasted mergansers will sometimes work together in a small flock to drive a school of fish into the shallows, where they are more easily trapped. The backward-pointing serrations along the mergansers' narrow bills are well suited for catching and holding their slippery prey.

Along the Mashomack shoreline, large rafts of sea ducks ride the sea swells and dive as much as forty feet to reach shellfish beds. Sea ducks include all three species of North American scoters—the white-winged being the most numerous, then the surf scoter and the common, or black, scoter. These large sea "coots" (as hunters refer to them) have powerful gizzards that crush hardshell clams and other shellfish that they have swallowed whole.

Then there are the garrulous oldsquaws. They abound in nearby Gardiner's Bay and Shelter Island Sound, where they call and chatter incessantly.

Listen through the chilling air, and you will hear the sounds that author Peter Matthiessen heard with his boatman father as a boy growing up. In these waters of the Peconic Bay, he has written, he learned to swim, fish, and handle small boats, and "a lifelong fascination with wild birds and marine life had its start." —J.B.

OSPREY

If there is one creature that represents the wild spirit of Mashomack, it would be the osprey. Mashomack's unusual mix of tidal wetlands, surrounding bays, and tall oak trees makes it an ideal nesting place for the osprey, a large brown-and-white bird that feeds almost exclusively on fish.

The osprey, or "fish hawk," as it is also known, became threatened in the eastern and northern United States when chemical pollutants accumulated in fish and development encroached on the osprey's nesting habitats. However, improved water-quality standards, the ban on DDT, man-made nesting platforms, and successful reintroduction programs have all contributed to increased numbers in recent years.

In the summer of 1996, The Nature Conservancy tracked an osprey named X5 as she flew, with a transmitter tied to her back, from the Conservancy's Mashomack Preserve to the Pantanal Wetlands in Brazil. Ten days after X5 left Mashomack, satellites spotted her on Sapelo Island, Georgia. A few days later, she left Key West, Florida. In early September she flew over Haiti, and within a week she had crossed the Caribbean en route to South America. After flying over Venezuela and through Amazonia, X5 ultimately found her way to the Pantanal Wetlands in Brazil.

The Pantanal area of Brazil is the world's largest wetland and one of the world's most productive habitats. Healthy populations of jaguars, giant anteaters, and anacondas still roam here; millions of waterfowl breed here; and for several months of the year, X5 and other migratory birds feed here.

However, the stunning loss of habitat along the way has made this annual journey exceedingly difficult for many migratory birds. As they take flight each fall, some species must fly for up to one hundred hours before reaching the few and far between rest stops. Many of these stops are disappearing, plowed under by bulldozers and new resort developments. And in the Pantanal Wetlands, agriculture, deforestation, uncontrolled gold-mining operations, and illegal poaching are depleting the region's wildlife.

To address this problem, the Conservancy, along with the Wings of the Americas program (see page 87), made possible by Canon U.S.A., Inc., is taking a long-term, comprehensive approach to conserving key lands that support birds at risk throughout the Americas, so that X5 and other birds like her can continue their migrations and return safely to places like Mashomack each spring.

Winter Birds

WATERFOWL MIGRATION, VIRGINIA

On a cold, overcast January morning, the tidal Rappahannock River lies below a woodlands trail like a broad gray ribbon. Through an opening amid the tulip poplars and southern red oaks, a marshy cove comes into view. Its quiet waters are filled with wintering waterfowl.

Each fall thousands of ducks, geese, and swans descend upon the unspoiled coves, marshes, and swampy hardwood forests that line the lower Rappahannock. Fleeing colder weather in the Northeast, the Great Plains, and Canada, where they have spent the summer on their breeding grounds, these graceful waterfowl seek the open water of the Chesapeake Bay and its tributaries. Where surface ice forms, water birds cannot get to the underwater grasses on which they feed. But in these Virginia latitudes, ice is only an occasional and short-lived visitor.

The characteristic horseshoe-shaped bends of the broad, slow-flowing lower Rappahannock have formed thousands of acres of still-unspoiled freshwater marshes. Amid the big cordgrass, wild rice, arrow arum, and pickerelweed are numerous mallards, black ducks, ring-necks, Canada geese, and other migratory waterfowl. Less common are green-winged teal and pintails, both dabbling ducks. In the open water closer to the river's mouth are buffleheads, goldeneyes, and ruddy ducks. A thousand or more tundra swans are often seen, having completed a remarkable journey from as far afield as eastern Alaska and northern Canada.

The mysteries of such long-distance migrations are far from fully understood. Most birds migrate at night. They appear to find their way through a combination

RAPPAHANNOCK:
A NEW NATIONAL WILDLIFE REFUGE

It begins as a pure rushing stream in Virginia's Blue Ridge Mountains, races over falls near Civil War battlefields at Fredericksburg, winds by dramatic cliffs where bald eagles soar, slows and stretches miles wide as it rolls through the Tidewater, and finally empties into the Chesapeake Bay 184 miles from its start. The Rappahannock River is one of the Old Dominion's historic, recreational, and natural wonders.

The Nature Conservancy has been working to protect this marvelous resource since the 1960s and owns two preserves, the Voorhees Nature Preserve and Alexander Berger Memorial Sanctuary, along the river. It has recently joined together with other land trusts to help the U.S. Fish and Wildlife Service establish the Rappahannock River Valley National Wildlife Refuge. In 1998 the Conservancy acquired Toby's Point, a 364-acre riverfront parcel that includes a bald eagle nesting site, and will ultimately transfer it to the Fish and Wildlife Service. Through such joint efforts, it is hoped that the refuge will grow to 20,000 acres on the lower Rappahannock over the next several years—providing a critical refuge for the more than thirty thousand ducks, geese, and swans that winter on the river each year.

of hidden and visible cues—using stars and the earth's magnetic fields to navigate by night, the sun and such landmarks as shorelines and mountain ranges by day. While there are several competing theories as to how migratory behavior evolved, the common denominator behind all of them is food. In the main birds migrate not to avoid the cold but to find food.

Mallards are among the most abundant of the Rappahannock's seasonal visitors. The metallic-green head of the male makes it perhaps the most widely recognized of our ducks. The brown female, always by his side, is beautiful in her own right. Widely hunted, these ducks are wary, and it is a stirring sight to see a flock leap from the still water into flight, their wings *whup-whupping* as the alarm call sounds, off to settle in a nearby cove out of sight of the bird-watcher.

Also common are Canada geese, unmistakable with their black heads and necks and white chinstraps. About fifteen thousand individuals congregate on the river each winter. The V-shaped line and honking chorus of migratory geese far above is a sure sign of coming cold. While year-round resident geese have become troublesome pests to some in suburbia, these migrant flocks still appear as true emblems of wildness.

On this day, the waters of Owl Hollow Marsh reveal other treasures. A half dozen hooded mergansers float nobly amid the mallards. To some observers, the female, with her ruffled reddish crest, is even more beautiful than the male, with his remarkable fan-shaped white crest on a black face.

As the mallards take flight, you notice that a lone bird has remained behind, as if scornful of its companions' nervousness. With its chestnut-red head and neck, long sloped bill, and black chest and tail feathers bracketing a bright white body, this duck momentarily startles the viewer with its grace. It is a canvasback. After a long minute of quiet display, it too alights, flying upriver, away from where the mallards went.

All of these birds seem nearly wanton in their beauty, as if nature has designed each species not simply for its own utility but so that we might take pleasure in observing it.

—R.R.

Winter Woods

WINTER IDENTIFICATION WALKS, INDIANA

In the winter woods, it is impossible to identify different tree species in the most obvious way—the leaves. So by the end of The Nature Conservancy's winter hikes through Indiana's Saalman Hollow, all participants will have learned how to identify a tree a different way—by the bark.

In fact, the bark is one of the most accurate ways to identify a tree. Trees, in a sense, are like people. Their leaves are like hair. They change by season, by health, by how many nutrients they've received in the past months. Just as hair can be cut or dyed, leaves can also change color or fall off. But the face of the tree is the bark. Regardless of season, age, or health, a tree's bark remains remarkably the same throughout its life.

As the hikers start out, most think that many of the trees, without leaves, look similar. But slowly they begin to see the differences: the beech tree has smooth bark, like skin, with no ridges or furrows. The hornbeam looks the same at first; but under its smooth,

unfurrowed bark, this tree is ridged with what looks like corded muscle, making it easily recognizable from the beech.

Another common way to differentiate between trees is to cut into the bark. (Contrary to popular opinion, cutting shallowly into the bark does not hurt the tree.) Though the thick, widely ridged barks of the black walnut and sassafras trees look extraordinarily similar, when they're cut, the inside of the black walnut is revealed as a rich chocolate brown, and the sassafras is a startling orange.

It is even possible to identify these trees by smell: the black walnut tree does smell like a walnut shell, and the sassafras does smell fruity, like sassafras tea.

These 100 wooded acres are filled with more than fifty species of trees and shrubs, including American sycamore, white ash, American elm, papaw, yellow poplar, and sugar maple. At the northern end of the woods, hikers walk through a narrow entranceway into a dramatic box canyon of sandstone ledges and house-sized boulders. The canyon was formed by the waterfall at the top of the canyon and by the stream winding down out of the canyon's sandstone walls. In the most dramatic winter weather conditions, the waterfall and creek freeze over and icicles dangle over the ledges and overhangs.

If they're lucky and it's snowed recently, hikers can identify the tracks of animals that are active here in winter, including white-tailed deer, gray squirrels, fox squirrels, red and gray foxes, white-footed mice, deer mice, mink, raccoons, wild turkeys, and quail. Many tracks tell dramas: for instance, deer mice tracks, appearing in the snow as two parallel dotted lines with a scuff in the middle when the mouse drags his tail, might abruptly end with two solid wing marks in the snow—most likely belonging to an owl who just ate its dinner.

No matter what the weather conditions are within the woods, participants on the Conservancy's hikes find that there is always plenty to see and learn here. Though the woods are seemingly stark and lifeless in winter, they are actually teeming with activity just waiting to be discovered and observed. —P.H.

WINTER

During the cold winter months, many of us retreat to the fireside to wait for spring. But the more adventurous at heart will discover that nature is not missing from winter; it is just a little harder to find. By attuning your senses, developing a critical eye, and listening in the silence, you will find that life is still out there, waiting to be discovered.

Contrary to popular belief, winter does not purge the world of color. Although the colors of winter are subtler and must be sought out, they are rich and bold. Explore the color of the woods: from deep green moss growing on maroon bark to the sky's unsettling purples to the sun's reflections off ice crystals. After a light snowfall is the best time to look for the tracks of animals venturing out of their winter dens. When the ground is moist and the drifts of snow are not so deep as to distort the prints, it is possible to see signs of squirrels, rabbits, or perhaps even a fox or coyote that has passed the spot where you now stand. Study the branches of the trees above you and discover the birds' nests that are normally hidden behind thick foliage. The muted tones of winter allow for the discovery of nature that is concealed by the busyness of other seasons.

Likewise, the quiet in wintertime gives us the opportunity to listen more. Now the tumbling stream is muffled by strangling ice, an occasional bird cry echoes through the leafless trees, and the wind does not rustle branches but whistles between empty bows. Winter allows us to appreciate silence, to listen to our own footsteps, and to focus on our thoughts and meditations.

Annual Feast

BALD EAGLE ROOST, WASHINGTON

With powerful wings up to seven feet wide, the bald eagle (*Haliaeetus leucocephalus*) dives toward the riverbank for his morning meal of chum salmon. He grabs the fish with sharp, extended talons and rips it to pieces with his beak.

Around him in the winter chill, hundreds of eagles keep sharp eyes peeled for their next meal. On clear days, when warm air rises from the valley floor, the birds catch updrafts and soar in ever-widening circles above the river.

The bald eagles return here each winter, to the banks of Washington's Skagit River, where The Nature Conservancy and its partners have protected over 6,000 acres of prime bald eagle wintering habitat. The eagles begin to arrive in November, and their numbers gradually build to several hundred, peaking in mid-January, making this one of the four largest assemblies of bald eagles in the lower forty-eight states.

It is not by coincidence that this assembly coincides with the annual return of spawning chum salmon.

Thousands of these mature fish make the long upstream journey from the ocean, returning after four years to the freshwater tributaries of their birth. Their faded rosy bodies are battered and torn from the trip, and they expend the last of their energy to spawn in the Skagit River shallows. Once they are spawned out, they die, and their rotting carcasses wash up on the gravel banks and bars.

The eagles feast daily on the remains littering the banks. The birds are loud, feisty, and competitive as they swoop down from their perches in the cottonwoods, alders, and conifers lining the banks to gorge themselves. Squabbles erupt occasionally, as impertinent juveniles try to snatch salmon from their elders. Amid flapping wings, jumping, whistling, and squealing, the young eagles are put in their place and made to wait their turn.

The birds generally dine in the morning and spend the afternoon perched, until they begin again with a midafternoon feeding. Visitors to the Skagit River Bald Eagle Natural Area can observe the feedings from two roadside viewing areas.

When dusk begins to settle on the Skagit, the eagles slowly begin to desert the riverbanks and fly to their night roosts. Barnaby Slough, around which the Conservancy owns 151 acres, is one communal night roost. Here in the protective forest they roost on the branches of mature cottonwoods, alders, and big-leaf maples.

—P.H.

SAVING THE AMERICAN BALD EAGLE

Like winds and sunset, wild things were taken for granted

until progress began to do away with them.—Aldo Leopold

The bald eagle, our national symbol, is truly an all-American bird—it is the only eagle unique to North America. Though Benjamin Franklin thought the turkey was the best bird to represent the United States, Thomas Jefferson lauded the eagle as "a free spirit, high soaring and courageous." And most people agreed with Jefferson; in 1792 the bald eagle became the national symbol of freedom and independence.

In Thomas Jefferson's time, hundreds of thousands of bald eagles lived in the United States. But by 1963 its population in the lower forty-eight states had dwindled to fewer than one thousand nesting birds. Four years later, the bald eagle was classified as a federal endangered species in forty-three of the lower forty-eight states.

The eagle had suffered from hunting, loss of food and habitat, and contamination of its food sources. Logging, dam building, and pollution had decimated its nesting habitat and food supply. DDT and similar pesticides had contaminated its remaining food, causing sterility and interfering with its ability to develop sufficiently strong eggshells. Many eagles had also died of lead poisoning after eating prey that had been shot with lead shotgun pellets. Human disturbance had also played a role. When eagles were disturbed by nearby human activity, they fled their nests, leaving their eggs and babies exposed.

Since then, government agencies, conservation groups, and private citizens have banded together to save the bald eagle. Dam locks were built to keep sections of rivers from freezing over, so that the eagles would have new winter feeding areas. DDT was banned in 1972. States passed laws to require hunters to use nontoxic shot. Lands were set aside and protected for eagle feeding and nesting sites. And the eagle was recolonized in many states through reintroductions.

The eagle has made a miraculous comeback. In 1999, President William Jefferson Clinton took the bald eagle off the endangered list, reclassifying its status to threatened. Today, there are more than eight thousand nesting bald eagles in the lower forty-eight states, and the population is doubling every six to seven years.

Counting for Conservation

CHRISTMAS BIRD COUNT, IDAHO

Counting crows. And then house sparrows. Starlings.

And then, "Accipiter."

"Where?"

"Eleven o'clock in that large oak. Dark head. White eye stripe. Light underparts—"

"—I see it."

"Goshawk?"

"Northern goshawk. Nice spot."

Christmas Bird Counts go like this. Hours (often cold hours) traipsing about, counting large congregations of common birds such as crows and starlings, punctuated by the sudden appearance of something grand or surprising.

The National Audubon Society Christmas Bird Count, as it is officially known, has been going on since 1900; in 1998 nearly fifty thousand people turned out throughout North America, the Caribbean, Latin America, and the Pacific Islands to count birds—one by one, if possible. The count has been called the oldest and largest wildlife survey in the world. The field data it produces, along with the data gathered during the North American Breeding Bird Survey each June, provides a status report of the population of birds. The conservation applications of such data, as you might expect, are significant. According to the Audubon Society, the Christmas Count has brought attention to 115 species of birds that have declined significantly over the years.

Volunteers, often in teams, spread out to the nooks and crannies of North America and elsewhere to record species and numbers of individuals during a twenty-four-hour period sometime during the two and a half weeks surrounding December 25. Watchers count birds with both a sense of conservation and one of competition, comparing their results with others within their immediate counting area—a 15-mile-diameter circle (177 square miles).

One place in particular that has an exceptionally good Christmas Count is the Hagerman Valley in southern Idaho, at The Nature Conservancy's Thousand Springs Preserve.

Thousand Springs is an island and mainland on the Snake River. The combination of cliffs and open, swift-moving water makes it an ideal habitat for overwintering waterfowl and birds of prey, such as bald and golden eagles, northern harriers, and American kestrels. Tens of thousands of waterfowl are found here, and the Christmas Count typically nets between forty-five thousand and sixty thousand individual birds of all kinds, with some eighty species represented. For such numbers, counting individuals isn't feasible, so birders have to estimate the throngs of green-winged teal, mallards, ring-necked ducks, and American coots on the Snake.

The massive rafts of waterfowl contrast with the rare, lone bird that lucky counters see in any given year, such as, at Thousand Springs, the ferruginous hawk, mountain bluebird, golden eagle, or tufted duck. The tufted duck is especially remarkable, since its homeland is Eurasia and its appearance one Christmas in Idaho was, in birder's parlance, an "accident."

The tufted duck, incidentally, looks a lot like the ring-necked duck, of which counters marked 5,641 one year. The lesson here is a birder's verity: Assume nothing and glass everything.   —J.K.

CHRISTMAS COUNT (AND WINTER) BIRDING TIPS

Rick Blom, a twenty-five-year birder, a teacher, and a columnist for *Bird Watcher's Digest,* suggests these five tips for winter birding:

1. Find the feeding flock. If the winter woods are quiet, then you're in the wrong place. Birds such as chickadees, finches, juncos, and nuthatches tend to form feeding flocks during winter. Find the flock by walking around and listening carefully. The noisier birds, such as chickadees, will lead you to the flock. Take your time and have a good look: these flocks can yield unexpected bonuses, such as common redpolls and other winter migrants.

2. Patience. The birder's "psshhtt" brings birds out of thickets, so that each of you can get a better look at the other. But certain bird species respond more quickly than others. The busy chickadee tends to flush right away at a good "psshhtt." Stand still. Wait a bit. See what else might pop out. You might be surprised.

3. Get out of the wind. Birds don't like cold winter winds any more than you do. Find areas out of the wind, sheltered by trees, a hedgerow, a building. These areas, especially if they're in direct sun, often attract concentrations of birds.

4. All fields are not alike. A grassy field that is attracting northern harriers and red-tailed hawks during the day signals a healthy rodent population; it is a good place to be in the late afternoon when short-eared owls appear seemingly from nowhere, replacing the diurnal hawks, to work the same field during the second shift.

5. Backyard feeders. Twenty million people have backyard feeders, providing a boon for hungry winter birds and a good site for birding as well. Not only are seedeaters attracted to the feeders, but the eaters of seedeaters are as well—Cooper's hawks and sharp-shinned hawks, in particular, will stake out feeders, hunting the smaller birds.

River in Winter

WINTER ON THE CONSUMNES RIVER, CALIFORNIA

The Consumnes River Preserve in California's Sacramento County, at the eastern edge of the Sacramento–San Joaquin Delta, is the largest free-flowing river in the Central Valley. Though it is located nearly one hundred miles inland from the Pacific Ocean, the ebb and flow of its waters are affected by ocean tides funneling into the delta through San Francisco Bay. There are no major dams on the Consumnes, and heavy winter rains bring frequent flooding. The rich, dark silt carried by the floodwaters introduces valuable nutrients to the neighboring wetlands and grasslands, and the cycles of life renew themselves each year in the bright California sunshine.

The Consumnes is a river for all seasons. In the winter, the marshes ring with the haunting calls of greater and lesser sandhill cranes. Ross's, white-fronted, and Canada geese, tundra swans, and numerous species of ducks fill the air with their raucous cries. The preserve is full of the sound of wind and water. Thousands of birds stop here as they navigate the ancient air currents of the Pacific Flyway. The elegant, graceful sandhill cranes have spent their winters in and around California's Central Valley since at least the last ice age. The grasslands and agricultural fields provide foraging ground for the birds. In the pale light of sunrise, they take to the air, flying in graceful, swooping arcs, holding their necks out straight as they fly. Eventually, they break into smaller groups to begin feeding for the day—hunting carefully among the dry grasses, using their long, slender beaks to turn up insects and worms. They also eat grain left over from the harvest and hunt for frogs, snails, and mice in damp pastures.

A few minutes after sunset, as twilight settles and deepens across the gentle ripples of the Consumnes River, the sky fills again with the cranes returning to their roosts. Their haunting cries echo across the water and the forests as they have for thousands of years.

John Muir once described the lush streamside forests of the Consumnes River as a "tropical luxuriance." The great heights of the valley oak and Fremont cottonwood trees are laced with the graceful loops and trailing vines of wild grape. The massive oaks along the Consumnes owe their size (often seven feet in diameter and more than one hundred feet in height) to the richness of the seasonally flood-fed river. It is believed that many of the largest oaks were here when John Sutter first explored the river in the 1840s. Four species of willows bend their limber branches toward the water, and the edges of the river protect thick stands of Oregon ash, box elder, and button willow.

The forests gently give way to freshwater marshes, and in the drier areas of the preserve, grasslands thrive amid cultivated fields. More than two hundred species of birds have been recorded in and around the preserve, including several nesting pairs of majestic Swainson's hawks, diving and hunting in the clear skies above the river. But the cool heart of the Consumnes River Preserve is the river itself. The Consumnes runs with the thick, shiny bodies of salmon and steelhead. River otters splash and float in the smooth water, and muskrats make their homes along the sheltered banks.

—C.B.

CRANE DANCING

Scientists believe that cranes have inhabited the earth for at least sixty million years; the sandhill crane has been dated back nine million years. In many cultures, cranes carry special significance. In Japan they are honored as symbols of long life and happy marriage. In Vietnam they are believed to carry the souls of the dead to heaven.

Cranes typically mate for life and begin reproducing in their third or fourth year. They are social birds, and this behavior is evident in flight and on the ground. During landings and takeoffs, they constantly vocalize and call to one another. Although it is not proven, it seems that cranes do recognize the calls of mates and family members. Occasionally, a lone bird separated from its group can be seen flying back and forth over roosting flocks, calling out over and over again.

Among the most complex and fascinating of crane social behaviors is "dancing." Often seen among new or recent pair bonds, crane dancing can occur at any time of year and among birds of all age groups. The crane lowers its head while lifting and spreading its wings, then suddenly raises its head and lowers its wings, sometimes jumping at the same time. The bird may also pick up and throw sticks or small plants. The behavior tends to be contagious, and a period of intense dancing may spread quickly through an entire social group.

On a Winter Breeze

RARE BIRDS, ARIZONA

In all America such magic places are few.

—EDWIN WAY TEALE
ON THE PATAGONIA–SONOITA CREEK PRESERVE

Not long ago, an annual Christmas Bird Count at The Nature Conservancy's Patagonia–Sonoita Creek Preserve in southeastern Arizona turned up a bird that shouldn't have been there. It was the blue mockingbird (*Melanotis caerulescens*), a secretive, sapphire-colored *avis,* and it was some two hundred miles from its nearest relatives in Mexico. What makes this more unusual is that blue mockingbirds don't migrate.

Word spread quickly, and before long, bird enthusiasts from New Jersey to California had come to see the mockingbird, whose normal range is the lowlands and mountains from southern Sonora to southwest Chihuahua, and southern Tamaulipas to the Isthmus of Tehuantepec. The mockingbird stayed on at Patagonia–Sonoita through the new year.

And so it often goes at the Conservancy's 750-acre Patagonia–Sonoita Creek Preserve, a stream-fed oasis of cottonwood-willow forests, *cienagas* (wetlands), and sacaton grasslands situated between the Patagonia and Santa Rita Mountains, twenty miles from Mexico. You never know what might wing in on a winter breeze.

One year, in a similar surprise sighting, another tropical native came north, far out of its range: a crescent-chested warbler (*Parula superciliosa*). The crescent-chested, aptly named for the red splotch on its bright yellow underbelly (it's also known as the spot-breasted warbler), was first seen on the outskirts of the preserve near the quiet village of Patagonia, and it stayed in the vicinity for several months. Indeed, for two consecutive wintry seasons the bird traded its life in the high pine-oak and cloud forests from Mexico to Nicaragua for the towering cottonwoods and craggly willows along Sonoita Creek.

Such unusual company at the preserve raises the question, Why would these Mexican birds, which do not migrate, come north in winter? While ornithologists have found no definitive answer, in the view of most, the simplest explanation may be the best: the birds sometimes get off track.

During a typical January week the preserve's "birds of note" roster includes upward of forty species, among them rare visitors from the eastern U.S., such as the eastern phoebe (*Sayornis phoebe*) and the black-and-white warbler (*Mniotilta varia*), a warbler that slinks along branches and tree trunks like a nuthatch.

Still another Mexican species, the rufous-backed robin (*Turdus rufopalliatus*), occasionally visits in January and February. A slightly paler gray version of its cousin, the American robin (*Turdus migratorius*), the rufous-backed has a red sash over its shoulders and a more prominently streaked throat. Somewhat secretive, these birds can sometimes be seen in the dense shrubs and treetops of the preserve.

And the list of rarities goes on (more than 275 species have been reported here throughout the year). As the naturalist Joseph Wood Krutch observed of the refuge, "It is alive with birds of astonishing variety." And it rarely disappoints. —T.B.

BIRDING SOUTHEASTERN ARIZONA

Southeastern Arizona is a bird-watcher's paradise at any time of the year. At the axis of two major deserts and several mountain ranges along the border with Mexico, this corner of the state has a plethora of habitats for avifauna, and breathtaking vistas for all.

Over a long weekend, birders can visit several premier birding locales within a few hours of Tucson. One possible itinerary includes The Nature Conservancy's Ramsey Canyon Preserve in the wooded foothills of the Huachuca Mountains. Here, hummingbirds are the main summer attraction (more than fifteen species regularly visit), but other possibilities are buff-breasted flycatchers, Strickland's woodpeckers, and olive and red-faced warblers. In the winter, within a few hours' drive of the preserve, one can find two out of three of all the sparrow, bunting, longspur, and towhee species in the entire United States.

Also from Ramsey Canyon, an easy drive to the east is the San Pedro Riparian National Conservation Area. Walking among the willows and cottonwoods along the San Pedro River, birders may glimpse gray and Swainson's hawks, green kingfishers, and summer tanagers, to name a few of the more than 375 species reported in the area. Two other small mountain ranges, the Santa Rita and Chiricauha, are also world-class sites; there birders can sometimes glimpse elegant trogons, painted redstarts, and rose-throated becards, among others.

Armies of the Night

DESERT LIFE, ARIZONA

What draws us into the desert is the search for something intimate in the remote.
—EDWARD ABBEY

In the half-light of dusk in the canyon, saguaro cacti (*Carnegiea gigantea*) look eerily like giant soldiers on the march, with multiple arms akimbo or raised in greeting. There are hundreds of them. They outnumber you as night falls and the moon rises.

These aggregations of saguaros are sometimes called "forests," alluding to the concentration and number of these giant cacti and how they tower above all else in the desert landscape.

Unlike other cacti, such as prickly pear, which is present in the other North American deserts—the Chihuahuan, Great Basin, and Mojave—the saguaro is a stay-at-home species, found only in the Sonoran Desert. The Sonoran, one of the continent's hottest and driest regions—even in winter— covers 120,000 square miles from southern Arizona west to south-eastern California and south to Mexico. The saguaro, which can live two hundred years, grow to fifty feet, and weigh twelve thousand pounds, is so strongly identified with the Sonoran that its blossoms are the state of Arizona's official wildflower.

The saguaro does not like cold. This is illustrated quite obviously in Aravaipa Canyon. In Aravaipa, as you hike along the trail that dips in and out of the cool, willow-lined Aravaipa Creek, saguaros line the steep hillsides along your way. Other cacti, such as cholla, fishhook, and prickly pear, grow among the saguaros. But about midway through the canyon, as you head farther east, the saguaros suddenly stop—as though there is a line in the sand they won't or can't cross. The line is the eastern ecological edge of the Sonoran Desert. Go any farther to the east and you emerge into a semidesert grassland of higher elevation. And though it didn't feel like it as you hiked through the canyon, the elevation from the trailhead at 3,000 feet to this point has climbed more than 500 feet. And saguaros don't like height or its attendant cold. They will not grow here.

Instead, saguaros typically stick to elevations below 3,500 feet. So well adapted is the saguaro to the Sonoran that 95 percent of this cactus is water. If enough water is available, a mature saguaro can add a ton to its weight expeditiously. Not only does the cactus store water in its stems, but it secretes a thick, waxy layer that virtually waterproofs itself and prevents water loss.

The plant is also an important source of food and shelter for other creatures of the desert. Many birds rely on the saguaro. Gila woodpeckers, gilded flickers, and owls will nest in cavities in the cacti, while red-tailed hawks and Harris's hawks will nest atop the prickly arms and trunk. Long-nose bats are pollin-ators of the saguaro at night, as is the white-winged dove during the day. Hosts of birds, rodents, and armies of ants and other invertebrates—vastly out-numbering the armies of saguaros—eat its fruit.—J.K.

DESERT ETIQUETTE

➤Stay off the cryptobiotic soil. It is dusky-colored and looks inert; it is not. Cryptos are the linchpin of certain desert ecosystems, and trampling them causes erosion that in turn harms plants and water sources.

➤Don't collect anything: wild plants, Native American artifacts, petrified wood, or fossils.

➤Don't build fires.

➤Don't touch cacti or other desert plants—for their sakes and yours. Many sting, are barbed, or are poisonous, and they're that way for a reason.

➤Don't disturb water sources. Streams, springs, and water pockets are precious surface-water providers for wild animals. Don't pollute these and don't hang around them for long periods, thereby discouraging others who are thirsty from visiting them.

➤Pack it in, pack it out.

➤Have fun!

Wing-Footed

At the very tip of Long Island's South Fork, where Montauk juts out into the Atlantic, the January air is cold, damp, salty, and biting—perfect seal weather.

During low tide, harbor seals bask in the dim winter sunlight on the large, flat rocks off Montauk State Park. They dive into the sea, their dog-like, whiskered faces suddenly disappearing below the water's surface. Occasionally, lucky onlookers might also see a gray seal roll up out of the sea.

The seals are well adapted to the chilly air and water. Thick layers of blubber protect them from the cold, give them their characteristic streamlined shape, and make them efficient underwater swimmers. These roly-poly creatures may be awkward on land, but in the water they move with surprising grace and speed. Their high blood volume enables them to store enough oxygen to remain underwater for nearly half an hour.

Though seals normally shun areas that are populated by humans, they migrate here each winter to escape the colder waters farther north. In the last ten years, some seals have been reported to remain in the area year-round, though most just visit between November and May. They have trouble hauling out onto rocks during strong winds and high seas, so they wait for calm waters and southerly winds, which allow them to peacefully sun themselves for hours. They are found in several areas around the Peconic Estuary, including the rocks outside the Sag Harbor breakwater and the Shinnecock Inlet—both spots with abundant food and suitable resting places.

Harbor seals are the most common seal species seen off Long Island. With silvery gray to dark brown speckled fur, they grow to between five and six feet long. Males can weigh over 250 pounds. In the past ten years, gray seals have become more common in these waters, and Arctic harp and hooded seals are also seen here on occasion.

Though the frolicsome seals spend a lot of time hauled out, they actually devote most of their time to the pursuit of food. Their large teeth help them catch fish, which they swallow whole. Their eyesight is sharper underwater, helping them spot their prey in the murky underwater light. They feed on a variety of finfish and shellfish, including herring, mackerel, cod, whiting, flounder, squid, green crabs, and mussels.

All seal species are marine mammals. They breathe air and give birth to live young. Scientists believe they evolved from land mammals millions of years ago. As members of the Pinnipedia order, their relatives include sea lions and walruses. Their name is derived from the Latin words *pinna*, meaning "fin, flap, or wing," and *pedis*, meaning "foot." Thus, the pinnipeds are the "wing-footed" mammals of the sea.

Long Island's seals are "true" seals: they lack an external ear flap and have short stubby flippers. True seals use their rear flippers for propulsion and steer with their front flippers, while their relatives the sea lions use their front flippers to swim and steer with their rear flippers. While true seals are found here and northward in colder waters during winter, their sea lion cousins frequent warmer waters.

The Nature Conservancy is working to protect these waters in and around the Peconic Estuary. A scenic and biologically rich region, the watershed supports over 140 rare species and is designated as one of the U.S. Environmental Protection Agency's National Estuary Programs. Through such protection efforts, these waters should remain a haven for the wonderfully whiskered seals each winter. —K.C.

SEAL STRANDING

As seal populations rise in the waters around Long Island, so do seal strandings —when sick or injured seals become helplessly stranded on beaches or rocks.

Luckily, the Marine Mammal and Sea Turtle Stranding Program of New York State responds to any whale, porpoise, dolphin, sea turtle, or seal stranding on Long Island. If an animal washes up alive, medical assistance and care are given. The animal is eventually released back into the wild whenever possible.

Such a program is critical for these waters. In the first several months of 1998 alone, over fifty harp, hooded, and harbor seals were stranded. Since the Stranding Program was established in 1980, it has assisted over two thousand animals. As well as the many seals and sea turtles it has saved, the program helped the first and only successful rehabilitation and release of a baby sperm whale.

The Stranding Program, operated and supported by the Riverhead Foundation for Marine Research and Preservation, urges all people who find stranded sea turtles or other marine animals to keep their distance: all wild animals under stress may bite or be aggressive, and all carcasses may contain harmful bacteria. Determine the exact location of the animal and call for help.

At War with a Weed

ALIEN SPECIES REMOVAL, HAWAI`I

In January, it is hot and sticky on the Hana coast of Maui. But this doesn't stop a group of weary, mosquito-plagued *Miconia* hunters as they trudge through the rain forest on the windward slopes of Haleakala volcano. They are searching for the alien plant that has destroyed most of Tahiti's rain forests, the plant the Tahitians call the "green cancer."

Miconia calvescens is one of many destructive plant and animal species in the Hawaiian Islands. The alien species problem reaches back fifteen hundred years ago, to when the first Polynesian voyagers arrived on Hawai`i's shores, bringing with them plants and animals not native to Hawai`i. Europeans arriving in the late 1700s also brought several species destructive to the islands' native environment. Today, these species and hundreds of more recent introductions are the primary threat to the survival of Hawai`i's native ecosystems and species.

Miconia in particular has the potential to completely take over Hawaii's rain forests if left unchecked. This plant is easily identified by its broad green, velvety leaves with distinctive purple undersides. It grows so quickly, shooting up in tall, thin trunks from the floor of Hawai`i's rich rain forests, that natives like the ghostly, twisted `ohi`a trees are shaded out where they stand. A single mature *Miconia* tree can produce twenty-two million seeds a year, which are easily dispersed and quickly take root in Hawai`i's rich soils.

Volunteers from all over Hawai`i have joined the fight against *Miconia* and other alien plants. Day-trippers and hikers call in *Miconia* sightings to a local hotline. High school students give up many of their free Saturdays to find and remove alien plants. Other volunteers, including tourists who sacrifice days of lounging on Hawai`i's beaches, carry machetes and hike up through narrow streambeds, scrambling over slick, moss-covered boulders to search out and remove *Miconia* infestations. They spend hours hacking at the patches of thick plants and then pulling them out by the roots.

The ongoing fight against *Miconia* is a series of

small victories in the larger battle to save the islands' native plants and animals. Beneath the blazing blue sky, residents and visitors work tirelessly to protect Hawai'i's natural heritage. At the end of a long day of plant removal, they walk back down through the forest while listening for the calls of Hawai'i's rare and endangered forest birds. If they are lucky, perhaps a scarlet-colored 'i'iwi with its sickle-shaped bill or a crimson 'apapane will whir by their path before disappearing into the deep green forest. —M.R.

WHY IS HAWAI'I SO VULNERABLE?

Miconia calvescens is one of the more recent and well-publicized threats to Hawai'i's native species. However, many other alien species continue to besiege the islands and their complex web of natural communities and native ecosystems.

The Hawaiian Islands are the most isolated landmass in the world. For millions of years, two thousand miles of open ocean was a formidable enough barrier to isolate Hawai'i from the rest of the world. Plants and animals succeeded in crossing the ocean and colonizing Hawai'i perhaps as seldom as once every fifty thousand years. Those that survived the extraordinary journey found a pleasant climate, fertile soils, few competitors, and fewer diseases or predators. These colonizers, and the thousands of species that evolved from them, are Hawai'i's native species.

In a land with only two mammals (a bat and a seal), no reptiles, no land amphibians, and free of many diseases, many native species slowly lost the natural defenses that they would have needed if these elements were present. For example, many plants in continental ecosystems have poisonous saps or thorns as a defense against predators; most Hawaiian plants do not. And with no need to escape from large mammals, several native Hawaiian birds lost their ability to fly.

Having evolved on islands without large mammals, many native species cannot withstand the effects of pigs, goats, sheep, and deer. These hoofed animals inflict catastrophic damage by trampling vegetation and rooting up the tender shoots of young plants, opening the way for other, aggressive animal and plant pests. Mosquitoes, for example, spread avian malaria and pox, diseases that have devastated Hawai`i's native birds in many lowland areas.

Even greater threats stand poised to invade Hawai`i. Among them is the brown tree snake, which has already wiped out nine of Guam's eleven native land-bird species and most of the non-native birds as well.

Hawai`i's residents and visitors can help ensure that the snake and other species don't destroy the fabric of Hawai`i's natural environment by reporting pests via hotlines, volunteering on work trips, and spreading the word on how to protect Hawai`i's fragile native environment.

Wizened Elders

WILDHAVEN PRESERVE, OREGON

Their branches gnarled, their trunks twisted, the low-slung western junipers at Wildhaven Preserve are the wizened elders of the pine forest that rises around them. Some have stood for nearly one thousand years. Their contorted trunks are huge for a tree that measures just a foot in diameter after a century's growth.

And, remarkably, Wildhaven's junipers are still children; scientists estimate that the oldest individual trees of this species took root three thousand years ago in California.

By human standards, western junipers (*Juniperus occidentalis*) are all but immortal. They are the enduring heart of The Nature Conservancy's Wildhaven Preserve, a 160-acre inholding in the Deschutes National Forest in central Oregon. Even in winter, the preserve glows with the color and life that have grown up around them.

There is the reddish brown bark, the gray-green leaves, the unmistakable juniper scent of the trees themselves. Rock-hard branches support a chartreuse lichen that some say was once used to poison wolves. Today, it serves less sinister purposes, providing a dye favored by weavers and decorators.

The juniper's pea-sized, berry-like cones, however, are what draw the animals; more than eighty species, from mule deers to Townsend's solitaires, feed on the cones. In the fall, migrant robins, bohemian waxwings, and cedar waxwings flock around the area, looking for food. It is only in the true dead of winter that the Townsend's solitaires come down from the Cascade Mountains in search of sustenance and warmth. On mild winter days they fill the air with their metallic voices, their song a warning to other birds to steer clear of the solitaires' winter food supply.

The Townsend's solitaires find shelter in the forest, and they offer something in return as well. Passing through the bird's stomach, the juniper berries lose their fleshy covering, making them far more likely to germinate. The birds return the seeds to the ground, and new trees take root.

From time to time, gregarious pinyon jays join the

Townsend's solitaires, always returning from their travels to the juniper forest that serves as their year-round home. These social birds travel in large, loose flocks, and their nasal, mewing calls are a familiar sound to those who know this terrain. The trees provide thick branches to hold their nests, as well as those of the mourning dove, gray flycatcher, and Clark's nutcracker.

Hidden inside the cavities of these generous trees, pygmy nuthatches roost communally to escape the cold. Meanwhile, mule deer, worn out and looking for succor, browse the trees for berries and take shelter in the soft soil underneath.

For visitors both human and wild, there is solace in this ageless forest. At Wildhaven, centuries pass like hours. Generation after generation of mule deer, pinyon jays, and Townsend's solitaires return to find comfort from the bleakness of winter. While the outside world grows ever more frantic, the western juniper quietly endures.

—B.D.

MOUNTAIN NESTERS

A SHORT LIST OF BIRDS' NESTS OF THE EASTERN CASCADES

Birder's tip: Come spring, look up, look down, look all around (and listen)—only some birds nest in the trees.

BLACK-THROATED GRAY WARBLER (*Dendroica nigrescens*)

Very orderly cup-shaped nest of weeds, grass, and plant fibers lined with feathers, fur, hair, and moss.

Often rests far out on a limb of fir or oak, holding four speckled white to off-white eggs.

BROWN CREEPER (*Certhia americana*)

Usually in pockets where tree bark is sloughing off, especially on junipers. Five to six white eggs flecked

with auburn and held in hammock-like fashion atop bark, moss, needles, and silk.

CLARK'S NUTCRACKER (*Nucifraga columbiana*)

Like a cup and saucer, a platform of twigs and bark supports an inner bowl of bark, grass, needles, hair, and feathers. Up to six pale green mottled eggs. Always in coniferous trees.

GREEN-TAILED TOWHEE (*Pipilo chlorurus*)

Big, thick nests of grass, bark, twigs, and stems found on the ground to two and a half feet up in the shrubs. Eggs, usually three or four, are white and spotted with brown and gray.

TOWNSEND'S SOLITAIRE (*Myadestes townsendi*)

Often amid roots or in a shallow hole in the dirt, but also as high as ten feet up in a dead tree. White to light blue and brown eggs rest on a shallow bed of grass atop twigs and sticks.

WHITE-HEADED WOODPECKER (*Picoides albolarvatus*)

Built in a cavity of a dead or dying tree, usually pines, and lined with wood chips. Same tree—but different nest—may be used year after year, usually for four or five white eggs.

WILLIAMSON'S SAPSUCKER (*Sphyrapicus thyroideus*)

A cavity nest holding five or six white eggs. One bird will occasionally use the same tree for life, often a high-elevation aspen, pine, fir, or larch, excavating up to forty nests.

The Owls' Eyes Have It

WINTER OWLS, MICHIGAN

I rejoice that there are owls. They represent the stark, twilight, unsatisfied thoughts I have.
—HENRY DAVID THOREAU

Under a weak winter midday sun, a snowy owl sits on a fence post.

An owl at noon?

In the eastern Upper Peninsula of Michigan in February, a snowy owl is not an uncommon sight among the frozen fields and along the Great Lakes shorelines. The snowy owl, which hunts primarily lemmings on the Arctic tundra during long summer days, is essentially a diurnal species—that is, it is active during the day. Each winter the snowy appears in Michigan and across the northern tier of states from coast to coast and is quite comfortable in the daylight, unlike the majority of owl species.

Other Arctic and boreal species of owls appearing in the eastern Upper Peninsula, where The Nature Conservancy has a number of preserves, include the northern hawk owl, boreal owl, and great gray owl. State resident owls are the short-eared owl, long-eared owl, great horned owl, northern saw-whet owl, and barred owl. Two owls historically found in Michigan but not in the Upper Peninsula area are the eastern screech owl, which doesn't come this far north, and the barn owl, which is critically endangered in the state.

The variety and abundance of the order Strigiformes in the eastern Upper Peninsula make it one of the best places to "owl" in the country, according to *Birder's World* magazine. Among birders, "owlers" are a different lot. Like their quarry, they are often nocturnal. They also sound like their quarry, imitating owl calls in hopes of a wild response in the dark. And if they're owling in winter, they're bundled up so much that they resemble the bulk of the great gray. One of the appeals of owling in the eastern Upper Peninsula is that not only are the snowies out and about during the day, but great grays, northern hawk owls, boreals, short-eared owls, and even the odd barred owl can be seen in the sun.

Arctic and boreal species of owls appear here in what are known as "irruptions." Irruptions of owls in the States correspond, biologists believe, to scarcity of prey in their northern ranges in Canada. Populations of rodents and rabbits are cyclical; thus great grays, for example, appear in Michigan in good numbers in three- to five-year intervals. The winter of 1991–92 produced the greatest recorded number of great grays, with sixty—twice as many as ever before recorded.

Owls—especially one Michigan resident, the great horned owl—are predaceous in the extreme. Not only will this common "hoot" owl of the woods prey on mice, voles, and songbirds, it will also attack ducks, hawks, falcons, other owls, and even skunks—one of the few predators with the stomach for such meat. All owls are superbly specialized: the snowy owl's legs are feathered to ward off the Arctic tundra cold, and nocturnal owls, such as the barred, have large, frontally positioned eyes (like humans' but dozens of times more light-sensitive), highly sensitive ears, powerful talons and beaks, and feathers that are fringed in such a way as to make the owl nearly silent on the wing as it comes in for the kill.

For the resident owls, such as the great horned, February is a breeding month, with eggs already being incubated. Owlets typically fledge in late April and May, depending on the species. For the migratory species, as the ice breaks in the spring, owls, along with other boreal and Arctic birds, such as white-winged crossbills, boreal chickadees, snow buntings, rough-legged hawks, and gyrfalcons, will disperse into the sweeping coniferous forests and permafrost tundras of Canada, where they will breed.
—J.K.

OWLS AT A GLANCE

➤The smallest North American owl is not the pygmy owl but the elf owl—about the size of a sparrow.

➤The great gray is the biggest owl in stature but not in weight. It is lighter than the great horned owl and the snowy owl.

➤Owl calls have considerable variety. The barred owl is often represented in field guides as sounding like *"Who cooks for you? Who cooks for you, now?"* The saw-whet owl is named for its call, which sounds like filing or "whetting" a saw.

➤An owl can turn its head as much as 270 degrees to follow a moving object.

➤Screech owls vary their ranges according to food availability. A typical rural range may be from 75 to 100 acres. In urban areas the range shrinks to as small as 10 to 15 acres, since prey—birds, insects, and rodents—is more plentiful and concentrated.

Bird Communes

HERON ROOKERY, MARYLAND

Great blue herons (*Ardea herodias*) return every year around Valentine's Day to secluded nesting sites at The Nature Conservancy's Nanjemoy Creek Great Blue Heron Sanctuary. Here, among the lush wetlands near the Potomac River, the birds nest in communal rookeries high among the swaying branches of oaks, tulip poplars, and Virginia pine trees.

These rich, forested lands and healthy waters are home to one of the largest great blue heron colonies on the East Coast—about one thousand nesting pairs.

As the largest wading bird on the East Coast, the great blue heron stands four feet tall and has a six-foot wingspan. Perched atop thin, spindly legs, herons wade carefully through the shallow, dark waters, waiting to spear fish, frogs, and snakes with split-second jabs of their razor-sharp beaks. Their smooth, angular movements are strangely graceful as they stalk their prey.

Spring comes north with the herons and settles among the damp mists and wetlands along the wooded, swampy edges of the Potomac River. At the Nanjemoy Creek Sanctuary, the female herons lay their bluish green eggs in March. By May or June the colony is alive with the shrieks and screams and raucous cries of young herons clamoring for food. The forest rings like a tropical jungle. In July, the young herons are nearly adult-sized and are beginning to flex their wings. They perch carefully among the branches and flap their slate-gray wings tentatively, shifting their weight awkwardly from one skinny leg to the other. Soon they are swooping from tree to tree and preparing to begin the long autumn migration south.

The location of the nesting areas changes slowly over time. The herons are sensitive, and staff and visitors must be careful not to disturb them during nesting and breeding. They are very skittish and can be set to squawking and flurried activity by a single person walking in the woods. The nests they build are large platforms of sticks and twigs, slightly hollow and lined with a smooth layer of fine twigs. The nests stay in the trees all year, even after the herons are gone.

Every year in December or January, before the birds begin to reinforce their nests and while the tree branches are still bare and black against the winter sky, volunteers move quietly through the sanctuary to count and map the nest locations in order to track the size and shifting of the colony. Volunteers crane their necks and peer carefully among the leaves and branches to chart the nests. As few as one and as many as ten nests can be found in a single tree—a silent, but striking reminder of the sanctuary's lively springtime clamor.   —C.B.

DELMARVA BAYS

Delmarva bays, Maryland's small seasonal ponds, look nothing like their famous sister body of water, the Chesapeake Bay, a few miles to the west. You can't sail in them or scoop up crabs or kick up salty phosphorescent spray at night. However, an immense wealth of diversity thrives in and around the Delmarva bays, including rare plants and amphibians whose life cycles are tied to the constantly changing conditions of life in these shallow pools of fresh water that evaporate and fill with the seasons.

In a state that has lost 73 percent of its wetlands over the past two hundred years, Maryland's Delmarva bays are survivors and important conservation targets. With so much land drained and under cultivation on the eastern shore since the seventeenth century, it's amazing that the Delmarva bays exist at all. They are part of the phenomenon of coastal plain ponds, seasonally flooded upland depressions found in an arc from Massachusetts to Texas. On the Delmarva Peninsula—the conjunction of Delaware, Maryland, and Virginia—bays are generally found along its north-south "backbone," where fifty feet above sea level qualifies as upland.

Booming on the Prairie

COURTING PRAIRIE CHICKENS, TEXAS

When the "booming" begins on the Galveston Bay Prairie Preserve in Texas, it's a sure sign that spring is coming. The booming is the courtship song of the Attwater's prairie chicken (*Tympanuchus cupido attwateri*), one of the most endangered birds in North America.

The deep, low-pitched sounds echo like a chorus of woodwinds across the prairie at dawn. As the sun climbs over the horizon, they become faster, louder, and more urgent—until they can be heard miles away.

The songs signal the start of the Attwater's prairie chickens' annual courtship rituals. These rare birds, found only along the Texas Gulf Coast, gather on the tallgrass coastal prairie to act out a rowdy pageant of booming, dancing, foot stomping, whooping, and cackling—all performed by the males to impress the females.

The pageant occurs on the same leks, or booming grounds, year after year. The dominant older birds get center stage, leaving the younger males to stake out their territory in outlying areas.

The cocks warm up by stomping their feet and strutting across the lek to flaunt their brown-and-white plumage. Their neck feathers stand upright and their tail feathers are spread high and fan-like. They inflate and deflate their brilliantly gold-colored air sacs (tympana) on either side of their necks to make the booming sounds. Then the dance begins.

The leaping, hopping motion of the dance is at once chaotic and rhythmic. The cocks rise and fall, whoop, cackle, and strut for hours, until the sun is high in the sky. They leap straight up in the air and stop impulsively to burst into booming songs. These movements are said to have inspired Native American traditional dances.

The more dramatic the booming, the more the cock impresses the females, and one-upmanship among these demonstrative suitors is a loud affair. The females, on the other hand, make only quick, flirting appearances at the leks. Their calm demeanors and dull brown mottled feathers—blending nearly seamlessly into the wintered grass—set them apart from the flamboyant cocks. With practiced indifference, they walk leisurely around the lek until they choose their mate. Once they have made their choice and mated, they will not return to the leks until the next year. They disappear to build their nests in the tall grass, where they watch over their eggs until they hatch in April or May. Though they lay as many as twelve eggs each, the hens must watch carefully for egg-loving predators including fire ants, skunks, and raccoons.

The Attwater's prairie chickens currently exist in the wild at only three sites, including The Nature Conservancy's Galveston Bay Prairie Preserve—2,263 acres of protected tallgrass coastal prairie that also provides a home for wintering and migrating grassland songbirds, black-necked stilts, roseate spoonbills, and numerous other shorebirds and wading birds. The preserve is one of the last remaining safe havens for these threatened birds. —C.B.

ENDANGERED

Once the Attwater's prairie chickens were so plentiful that Native Americans could hear their booming calls all over the prairie. At the turn of the century, their population was thriving at over one million birds. As recently as World War II, booming birds had to be chased off runways before air force pilots could take off. At this time, the tallgrass coastal prairie habitat necessary for the birds' survival still stretched from northeastern Mexico into Texas and Louisiana.

During the past thirty years, however, most of this habitat has been lost to cattle grazing, farming, and urban and industrial development. Today this prairie is virtually gone; less than 2 percent remains.

As the habitat has diminished, the birds' numbers have swiftly declined. In the early 1990s, the Attwater's prairie chicken came precariously close to extinction. In 1996, only forty-two birds remained.

The species is now under the protection of the U.S. Fish and Wildlife Service. Groups, including The Nature Conservancy, have joined efforts to save this bird from the brink of extinction through captive breeding and habitat protection.

As part of this recovery effort, prairie chickens were hatched and raised in captivity at several zoos and wildlife centers. In 1996, nineteen of these birds were released onto the Galveston Bay Preserve to augment its existing prairie chicken population. More birds are released each year. Though many die from predators and other natural causes, over thirty birds have survived on the preserve, and fifty-six birds are estimated to exist in the wild. With growing support, the Conservancy and other groups are working hard to keep these exuberant birds booming and dancing.

A Lost World

RARE WILDFLOWERS, ALABAMA

Alabama's Little Cahaba River runs icy cold in late February. The trees beside its banks are still frost-veiled, the air is brittle, and patches of snow occasionally dot the ground. Yet on the glades nestled along the riverbank, the pale yellow flowers of the Alabama croton shrub have already begun to unfurl.

The flowers, growing in thickets, are as toxic as they are beautiful, and both wild animals and domestic cattle avoid them. Naturalists, however, treasure these delicate flowers because the Alabama croton (*Croton alabamensis*) is globally imperiled. Known as a "stay-at-home species," the croton grows here and along several other Alabama rivers—and nowhere else in the world.

The croton is just one of many rare and endangered species found here. The Cahaba River, Alabama's longest remaining free-flowing river, runs two hundred miles. It is home to exceptionally rich aquatic life: mussels, crayfish, snails, and 131 fish species—more fish species than are found in any river this size in North America. The river and its streams are full of white-water riffle areas where beds of aquatic plants thrive. Water willows, riverweeds, and the stunning Cahaba lilies will soon blossom out of the river's waters.

The Bibb County Glades run alongside the riverbank and through the surrounding woods. These open, limestone glades are home to one of the most significant concentrations of rare plant species in the Southeast. Their location, at the intersection of several different habitats, each with its own distinctive fauna and flora, has made the glades hotbeds of biological diversity. They contain such an assemblage of rare plants that they have been referred to as a "lost world."

Eight plant species previously unknown to science are found here. Also growing here are three federally listed species, ten candidates for federal listing, and seven species never before known to occur in Alabama—including one tiny flowering plant, the dwarf horse nettle (*Solanun carolinense* var. *hirsutum*), thought to be extinct since the early 1800s. In all, the glades are home to a remarkable sixty-one rare plant species.

February brings the first promise of spring to these riverbanks. The Alabama croton blossoms are still scattered and subdued, but already the bare twigs of red maple trees are developing red tinges, and soon their fruit will bloom. It takes only several weeks of longer, warmer days to produce the first flush of green growth on the ground and the precious, showy displays of yellow and white blossoms that shoot across the glade.—P.H.

EXTINCTION

Believe it or not, Alabama has lost more species of native plants and animals than any other state on the U.S. mainland according to the "1997 Species Report Card."

The report, compiled by The Nature Conservancy and a partnership of scientists across the U.S., is the most comprehensive appraisal of the health of native U.S. plants and animals. Its results are critical because every extinction brings with it an irreversible loss of unique genetic codes that are often linked to the development of medicines, foods, and jobs.

In Alabama, a land of ancient and complex geology and terrain and more than 235,000 miles of waterways, the freshwater life is exceptionally diverse. However, many of the state's rivers have been altered, and many species, particularly freshwater mussels and aquatic snails, are in danger of extinction. Twenty-four of Alabama's former inhabitants are already presumed extinct, with an additional seventy-four cataloged as missing and possibly extinct. Among its remaining species, more than one of every four is considered in danger of extinction.

The disturbing news is that the "Report Card" is not limited to Alabama. The report finds that one-third of all U.S. plants and animals are at risk of extinction. At least 110 U.S. plant and animal species have become extinct since the European discovery of North America, while another 427 are missing and may be gone forever.

Since the primary cause of species loss is habitat degradation or destruction, the Conservancy is working to protect critical habitat. The good news discovered over the past year is that seven species—including Alabama's dwarf horse nettle plant—thought to be extinct were rediscovered, leaving conservationists with hope for the future.

Appendix of Preserves and Protected Places

These preserves and protected places are open to the public—with some restrictions. You should phone ahead to check visiting hours and to learn if there are any closures due to sensitive conditions, such as nesting season. The primary purpose of these preserves is to protect biodiversity, and the Conservancy and its partners place this above all else as we manage these natural lands and waters.

ALABAMA

BIBB COUNTY GLADES
303 acres
(205) 251-1155

The Bibb County Glades are home to sixty-one rare plant species, including the dwarf horse nettle that was thought to have been extinct since the early 1800s. Eight of the plant species found on the glades have never before been known to science, including new species of rosinwood, blazing star, prairie clover, and Indian paintbrush. The Little Cahaba River that flows through the preserve harbors dozens of rare aquatic species, including the round rocksnail and the goldline darter. The glades are open to the public.

ALASKA

PRIBILOF ISLANDS
(800) 544-2248

The Conservancy's work on the Pribilof Islands involves financial and organizational support of the Pribilof Island Stewardship Program. While portions of the islands are accessible to the public, seals and other wildlife are easily disturbed by humans who come too close. All seal rookery and hauling complexes are therefore protected, and special blinds for visitors provide safe observation. The Native Corporation on the Pribilofs runs tours of the islands. Call for information.

ARIZONA

PATAGONIA–SONOITA CREEK PRESERVE
750 acres
(520) 394-2400

The Patagonia–Sonoita Creek Preserve is located within the narrow floodplain between the Santa Rita and Patagonia Mountains. The stream flows year-round, creating the cottonwood and willow corridor that lines its banks. The preserve is known worldwide as a prime birding area and draws more than twenty-five thousand visitors annually. More than 275 bird species have been sighted here, many of which range principally in Mexico (including the gray hawk). Elevation is

4,000 feet. The preserve has a visitor center with interpretative exhibits and materials, and is open to the public Wednesday through Sunday, year-round. Guided nature walks are given on Saturday.

RAMSEY CANYON PRESERVE
381 acres
(520) 378-2785

Visitors come from all over the world to see the 170 species of birds found on the Ramsey Canyon Preserve and surrounding national forest. Southwestern specialties such as painted redstarts and magnificent hummingbirds share the canyon with many other animals, including mountain lions, canyon tree frogs, four species of rattlesnakes, and dozens of butterfly species. The canyon is also home to more than four hundred species of plants, from tiny mosses to towering firs. The preserve is open to the public and currently hosts thirty thousand visitors per year. Its headquarters offer parking, a bookstore, and a bed-and-breakfast.

ARAVAIPA CANYON PRESERVE
42,000 acres
(520) 828-3443

Aravaipa Canyon is known by avid hikers as a smaller version of the Grand Canyon. Aravaipa Creek cuts a deep gorge through the Galiuro Mountains. Aravaipa is significant because of this flowing stream and its prime riparian corridor, which supports what is left of the best community of native fish in Arizona. The riparian corridor is also breeding habitat for a number of Mexican birds uncommon in the United States. A great portion of Aravaipa Canyon is Bureau of Land Management Wilderness land, which requires a hiking permit. For permit information, call the BLM Safford office at (520) 348-4400.

CALIFORNIA

CONSUMNES RIVER PRESERVE
6,700 acres
(916) 684-2816

Consumnes River is the only remaining undammed river on the Sierras' western slope. The benefits of its free-flowing course are many, yet most obvious is the creation of a floodplain that continues to sustain vital wetlands like those that were once common across the Great Central Valley. The preserve hosts tens of thousands of migratory Pacific Flyway birds and resident waterfowl, and supports some of California's largest virgin stands of valley oak and other streamside forests. Open daily to the public.

ELKHORN SLOUGH PRESERVE
388 acres
(831) 728-5939

This enormous coastal estuary located on Monterey Bay, the second largest in California, is not only verdant and fertile, it is vital. Every change in tide produces nearly twenty times more food than an equal area of open sea. More than 80 species of fish and 250 bird species are sustained here, including tens of thousands of migratory shorebirds that depend on the slough for necessary stopover feeding and resting. The Conservancy's Elkhorn Slough Preserve, which is open to the public, is adjacent to the 1,300-acre Elkhorn Slough National Estuarine Research Reserve. Programs at both properties are coordinated by the nonprofit Elkhorn Slough Foundation. Call for more information.

COLORADO

AIKEN CANYON PRESERVE
1,621 acres
(719) 632-0534

Bobcat country includes the 1,621-acre Aiken Canyon Preserve, located southwest of Colorado Springs. The preserve, open to the public, is one of the largest high-quality foothills ecosystems along the Front Range. The striking red outcroppings of the Fountain Formation welcome visitors to the canyon, which features rare pinyon-juniper woodland. Watch for more than a hundred species of birds, from golden eagles to hairy and downy woodpeckers.

PHANTOM CANYON PRESERVE
1,600 acres
(970) 498-0180

Phantom Canyon Preserve is a spectacular, roadless canyon, encompassing six miles of the North Fork of the Cache La Poudre River and an abundance of wildlife. Bald eagles use the canyon in winter months, and golden eagles and red-tailed hawks nest here. Guided field trips of the preserve are available by reservation from May to September.

The Conservancy's three preserves on the San Miguel River near Telluride cover ten river miles. The riparian forests are filled with songbirds, small mammals, and raptors. Along the canyon cliffs mountain lions roam, supported by an abundant deer population. The preserves are open to the public, and guided field trips are available.

CONNECTICUT

DEVIL'S DEN PRESERVE
1,746 acres
(203) 226-4991

Devil's Den is a patchwork of woodlands, wetlands, rock ledges, and a series of north-south ridges and valleys woven with streams and swamps. A wide variety of flora and fauna live on the preserve, including more than five hundred types of trees and wildflowers, the beautiful pink lady's slipper, cardinal flower, and Indian pipe among them. Devil's Den is home to the red fox, coyote, eastern copperhead, wood duck, ruffed grouse, pileated woodpecker, and more than 140 other bird species. The preserve features interpretive trails. Hawk hikes occur in the fall, and field hikes with natural historians occur throughout the year.

DELAWARE

FORT MAHON PRESERVE
341 acres
(302) 369-4144

This salt marsh is located at the mouth of the Mahon River, where it enters the Delaware Bay. In May and early June, it's a good viewing spot for horseshoe crabs and shorebirds including ruddy turnstones, red knots, semipalmated sandpipers, migratory sanderings, yellowlegs, dowitchers, and others. The preserve and the adjoining Little Creek Wildlife Area are open to the public and feature shorebird and waterfowl observation platforms.

FLORIDA

FLORIDA KEYS NATIONAL MARINE SANCTUARY
(305) 743-2437

The Conservancy works closely with the Florida Keys National Marine Sanctuary, which protects a barrier reef system that runs the length of the Florida Keys. Call the sanctuary for information. A good source of natural history information on the reefs and proper reef etiquette can be found through the Reef Environmental Education Foundation (REEF), which protects marine life through education, research, and involvement. Call (305) 451-0312 for information.

BLOWING ROCKS PRESERVE
73 acres
(561) 744-6668

Blowing Rock's mile-long beach is critical to nesting populations of threatened and endangered sea turtles. An array of shorebirds, brown pelicans, and ospreys rely on its sandy shore and ocean waters for food. On the west side of the preserve, mangroves along the Indian River Lagoon support small aquatic species such as blue crabs, shrimp, and juvenile fish. Endangered West Indian manatees seasonally inhabit the lagoon. The preserve is open to the public and offers educational exhibits, interpretive signs, a boardwalk, and trails.

GEORGIA

HARRIS NECK NATIONAL WILDLIFE REFUGE
2,765 acres
(912) 652-4415

The Conservancy helped protect the Harris Neck National Wildlife Refuge by buying sites and transferring them to the U.S. Fish and Wildlife Service to manage as part of the refuge. Approximately 1,500 acres is land, and the rest is salt marsh and freshwater ponds. The refuge is open to the public year-round. Not only does the spring bring good wood stork viewing (at a distance, so as not to disturb the rookery), but neotropical migratory birds are also plentiful.

HAWAI'I

KAPUNAKEA PRESERVE
1,264 acres
(808) 572-7849

Now part of the 47,000-acre West Maui Mountains Watershed Partnership, Kapunakea supports a wide array of communities ranging from nearly dry lowland forest at around 1,600 feet to wet montane forests and bogs at 5,400 feet near the summit. These diverse communities are home to a reported twenty-four species of rare plants, including five that are listed as endangered and four species of rare Hawaiian tree snails. Many of the plant species surviving in Kapunakea are integral to traditional Hawaiian cultural practices, such as hula and traditional medicine. Conservancy staff and volunteers lead interpretive hikes through the preserve. The trail is narrow, with sheer drop-offs in some places. Reservations and a deposit are required, and space is limited. Call for more details.

WAIKAMOI PRESERVE
5,230 acres
(808) 572-7849

Waikamoi Preserve is a sanctuary for hundreds of native Hawaiian species, many of them endangered or rare, and visitors are likely to catch a glimpse of rare native forest birds. Here, in windswept subalpine regions and rain forests of *koa* and *'ohi'a* trees, native plants, birds, and insects have woven an

ecological fabric like no other on the planet. The preserve is one piece in the seven-member East Maui Watershed Partnership that protects 100,000 acres of forest. Conservancy staff and volunteers lead interpretive hikes and volunteer work trips to the preserve. Reservations and a deposit are required for hikes, and space is limited. Call for more details.

IDAHO

THOUSAND SPRINGS PRESERVE
400 acres
(208) 726-3007

Thousand Springs Preserve forms a meandering ribbon of bottomland edged by basalt cliffs that follows the Snake River for more than two miles. It features the Minnie Miler Falls that cascade almost two hundred feet into a stunningly clear creek that flows into the Snake River. The preserve is open to the public Monday through Friday, spring through fall. Visitors are invited to walk a quarter-mile trail, tour the preserve's historic dairy barn, watch for birds, or canoe and fish the river. Festivals, hiking, and natural and cultural history field trips occur throughout the year, and the preserve hosts a Christmas Bird Count each winter.

ILLINOIS

THE LARUE SWAMP–PINE HILLS/OTTER POND
3,547 acres
(800) 699-6637

The LaRue Swamp–Pine Hills/Otter Pond is a Research Natural Area (RNA) within the Shawnee National Forest. RNAs are given the highest conservation protection status available in national forests. The Conservancy has worked on research projects here over the years and has purchased land that was incorporated into the national forest. Call for more information.

INDIANA

SAALMAN HOLLOW
100 acres
(317) 923-7547

Saalman Hollow is a scenic area of a hundred wooded acres, a small waterfall and stream, a significant sandstone cliff community, and a rare sandstone overhang community. Eight rare plants thrive here, including the nationally significant French's shooting star, Virginia saxifrage, farkleberry, mountain laurel, and shining clubmoss. The preserve is open to the public. Call for details.

IOWA

RICHARD W. POHL MEMORIAL PRESERVE AT AMES HIGH PRAIRIE
25 acres
(515) 244-5044

The Conservancy leases the Ames High Prairie from the Ames Unified School District. The preserve, featuring several remnant hillside prairies, was recently designated as a state preserve to afford it the highest protection status in the state. It is open to the public.

KANSAS

CHEYENNE BOTTOMS PRESERVE
7,269 acres
(785) 233-4400

Cheyenne Bottoms, the largest wetland system in Kansas, is the top shorebird staging area in the lower forty-eight states during the spring migration. Nearly 750,000 shorebirds, waterfowl, and wading birds visit the Bottoms each year. More than three hundred different species of birds—songbirds, raptors, and others in addition to the waterbirds—have been sighted at Cheyenne Bottoms, more than in any other location in Kansas. A self-guided tour is available of Conservancy and adjacent state wildlife area lands.

LOUISIANA

LAFITTE WOODS PRESERVE
10 acres
(225) 338-1040

Lafitte Woods Preserve is located on Grand Isle, Louisiana's only inhabited barrier island. The preserve is well known to birders as one of the most important migratory songbird stopover sites in coastal Louisiana. During spring and fall, a walk through the Spanish-moss-draped forest will reward visitors with views of countless warblers, tanagers, orioles, thrushes, and other migrant songbirds that pause to feed and rest during their passage to and from nesting and wintering grounds. The preserve is open year-round to the public during daylight hours.

MAINE

RACHEL CARSON SALT POND PRESERVE
77 acres
(207) 729-5181

The retreating tide exposes the quarter-acre salt pond where Rachel Carson gathered material for her book *The Edge of the Sea*. Today, children and adults alike discover long, slippery fronds of knotted wrack, blue mussels, hermit and green crabs, starfish, sea urchins, periwinkles, and other denizens of the intertidal and subtidal world. Salt Pond Preserve is located on the shores of Muscongus Bay. It is open to visitors, who are advised to consult tide charts before stopping by. Also, this is a delicate ecosystem, so please do not remove anything from the pond or leave any evidence of your visit behind.

MICHIGAN

JONATHAN WOODS PRESERVE
144 acres
(517) 332-1741

This biologically rich stand of hardwood forest shelters 289 plant species and 70 bird species. The preserve is open to the public year-round and is used extensively by the Seven Ponds Nature Center. Each spring, the Conservancy hosts field trips to hear and see eleven amphibian courtships.

MAXTON PLAINS PRESERVE
828 acres
(906) 484-9970

Maxton Plains Preserve, located on Drummond Island, is part of an eighty-mile stretch of northern Lake Huron shoreline that the Conservancy is protecting. Maxton Plains, a globally rare "alvar grassland," supports a unique mixture of Arctic tundra and Great Plains prairie plant species, including prairie smoke, Hill's thistle, false pennyroyal, and prairie dropseed. The mix of grassland, forest, and shoreline here attracts a multitude of butterflies and birds, including several owl species, ospreys, upland sandpipers, and northern harriers. The preserve is open to the public.

The entire northern Lake Huron shoreline and the area around Sault Ste. Marie, Michigan, are prime winter owling locales. Maxton Plains is one of several Conservancy preserves in the region. Call for more information.

MINNESOTA

SCHAEFER PRAIRIE PRESERVE
160 acres
(612) 331-0767

Beautiful displays of wildflowers are found at Schaefer Prairie. In all, the preserve's rich soils harbor more than 245 plant species, including the small white lady's slipper, Sullivant's milkweed (documented at only four other locations in the state), and the native Hill's thistle. A significant number of birds are found here, including the American goldfinch, bobolink, and common yellowthroat. It is one of the few places in the area where visitors can hear the ascending and descending whistle of the upland sandpiper, or the "pump-handle" creaking of the American bittern.

MISSISSIPPI

GULF ISLANDS
NATIONAL SEASHORE
135,625 acres
(228) 875-0821

Horn Island is part of the Gulf Islands National Seashore, a series of barrier islands that stretch 150 miles from Florida to Mississippi. To plan a trip to the barrier islands, contact the Gulf Islands National Seashore office in Ocean Springs, Mississippi.

MISSOURI

WAH' KON-TAH PRAIRIE
2,331 acres
(314) 968-1105

Wah'Kon-Tah is Missouri's second-largest prairie. The preserve is home to upland sandpipers, Henslow's sparrows, greater prairie chickens, and the scissor-tailed flycatcher. Regal fritillary butterflies sip nectar from Mead's milkweed,

and the endangered prairie mole cricket sings his courtship call in the twilight. The preserve is open to the public and hosts volunteer prairie-restoration days.

MONTANA

PINE BUTTE SWAMP
PRESERVE
18,000 acres
(406) 466-5526

Abutting the Bob Marshall Wilderness, some sixty miles southeast of Glacier National Park, the Pine Butte Swamp Preserve is at the heart of the largest wild expanse in the contiguous forty-eight states. The preserve features native foothills prairie, rocky ridges of limber pine and creeping juniper, spruce-fir forests, mountain streams, glacial ponds, and spring-fed swamp—providing prime habitat for a number of Montana's rarest native plants and animals. These lands are the grizzly bears' last stronghold on the plains. The Pine Butte Swamp Preserve is open to the public year-round and offers educational group tours and workshops. The preserve also features a guest ranch. Call for details.

NEBRASKA

NIOBRARA VALLEY
PRESERVE
56,000 acres
(402) 722-4440

The Niobrara Valley Preserve encompasses majestic pine-clad canyons, extensive grasslands, and a twenty-five-mile stretch

of the Niobrara River. There are two self-guided hiking trails on the preserve. Within a distance of less than a mile, hikers can experience several diverse ecosystems. The south trail passes through canyons of paper birch and eastern deciduous woodlands, tallgrass prairie, and marshes along the Niobrara River. On the north trail you will encounter floodplain, woodlands, mixed-grass prairie, and pine forest. The best time to visit is between May and September. Slide shows and bison tours are available by arrangement.

NEVADA

SPRING MOUNTAINS NATIONAL
RECREATION AREA
315,648 acres
(775) 873-8800

The Conservancy helped protect the endemic plants, animals, and natural communities of Kyle Canyon by working with the U.S. Forest Service and U.S. Fish and Wildlife Service on a conservation agreement for the Spring Mountains National Recreation Area. Call for visitor's information.

NEW HAMPSHIRE

FOURTH CONNECTICUT
LAKE PRESERVE
78 acres
(603) 356-8833

This northern New Hampshire preserve offers spruce and fir forests and a ten-acre bog. The preserve is open to the public, and hikers on the trail around the bog can see wildflowers in season and possibly a glimpse of moose in their natural habitat.

NEW JERSEY

CAPE MAY MIGRATORY BIRD REFUGE
212 acres
(609) 861-0600

The William D. and Jane C. Blair Jr. Cape May Migratory Bird Refuge is widely recognized as one of the East Coast's premier year-round birding spots. It offers a refuge for several species of owls, thousands of songbirds, and raptors including Cooper's hawks and peregrine falcons. Migrating dragonflies and butterflies also use the preserve to rest. In the spring and summer, endangered piping plovers and least terns breed on the beach. The preserve is open from dawn till dusk year-round and features a birding platform.

NEW MEXICO

GILA RIPARIAN PRESERVE
1,308 acres
(505) 988-3867

This preserve protects a prime example of fragile southwestern riparian habitat along the Gila River, one of the last free-flowing rivers in the American Southwest. The Gila is home to the most diverse broadleaf deciduous forests in New Mexico. One-third of all North American bird species have been sighted along this desert river. The preserve hosts Bell's vireo, the endan-

gered southwestern willow flycatcher, several rare fish species, and a host of other imperiled animal species. A portion of the preserve is open to the public.

NEW YORK

MASHOMACK PRESERVE
2,039 acres
(516) 749-1001

Mashomack Preserve on Shelter Island is one of the richest natural habitats in the Northeast. This preserve includes mature oak woodlands, interlacing tidal wetlands, freshwater marshes, and ten miles of coastline. A visitor center provides information about the seventeen-mile trail system, and a regular schedule of guided nature tours is provided to members and the public.

NORTH CAROLINA

BLACK RIVER PRESERVE
1,976 acres
(919) 403-8558

The oldest known trees east of the Rocky Mountains—a stand of 1,700-year-old bald cypresses—can be found on this meandering black-water stream. The Black River is a treat to canoe throughout the seasons. Visitors drift down the slow-moving, tea-colored stream flanked by stately bald cypresses draped with Spanish moss. Swamp roses bloom in the spring, and spider lilies grace the water in the summer. Spring is a good time to see

migratory songbirds nesting, while foliage is outstanding in autumn. The Conservancy offers canoe/camping weekends to the river. Call for details.

NORTH DAKOTA

JOHN E. WILLIAMS MEMORIAL PRESERVE
1,440 acres
(701) 222-8464

The John E. Williams Memorial Preserve supports not only sandhill cranes but hundreds of other migratory and characteristic species of the Great Plains. Rolling mixed-grass prairie and alkali lakes support the largest breeding population of the federally threatened piping plover anywhere in the United States. Other shorebirds and wildflowers are also abundant. The preserve is open to the public.

OHIO

EDGE OF APPALACHIA PRESERVE
12,000 acres
(937) 544-2188

The Edge of Appalachia Preserve is a nationally recognized preserve complex encompassing rugged woodland, prairie openings, waterfalls, giant promontories, and clear streams. Three areas—Lynx Prairie, Buzzardroost Rock, and The Wilderness—are registered National Natural Landmarks. Two areas—Lynx Prairie and Buzzardroost Rock—are open to the public. Call for details.

OKLAHOMA

TALLGRASS PRAIRIE PRESERVE
37,000 acres
(918) 287-4803

The Tallgrass Prairie Preserve offers sweeping vistas of open prairie, incredible sunrises and sunsets, and more than 750 species of plants and grasses including seasonal wildflowers. A diversity of grassland and forest habitats provides excellent birding. Greater prairie chickens boom in April and May. Numerous breeding neotropical migrant birds and birds of prey can be seen in the spring and summer, and bald eagles arrive in winter. The bison calving season runs from April through June. Other common wildlife species include white-tailed deer, bobcats, armadillos, beavers, woodchucks, badgers, coyotes, and numerous small mammals. The preserve is open dawn until dusk, every day of the year. From mid-March through November, the visitor center is staffed from 10 A.M. to 4 P.M.

OREGON

WILDHAVEN PRESERVE
160 acres
(503) 230-1221

In addition to some of the oldest western junipers in the state, Wildhaven Preserve includes ponderosa pine and a rare understory of bitterbrush grassland communities in excellent ecological condition. The species thrive in one of Oregon's driest regions—annual precipitation here is less than ten inches. The preserve was donated by Gil and Vivian Staender, who built a home by hand on the site and devoted their lives to conservation. Call for visitor's information.

DUNSTAN HOMESTEAD PRESERVE
1,222 acres
(503) 230-1221

Dunstan Homestead Preserve, a former ranch, extends four and a half miles along the Middle Fork John Day River. The river is key to recovery of wild salmon in the Columbia Basin.

Here at the preserve, habitat is being restored for salmon spawning as well as for the resident elk, beavers, songbirds, and other native wildlife. Alders, black cottonwoods, willows, and sedges create a diverse riparian community, while ponderosa pines and Douglas firs dominate the hills. The preserve is open to the public, and the best time to visit is May through November.

RHODE ISLAND

NATHAN MOTT PARK
40 acres
(401) 466-2129

Nathan Mott Park is located on Block Island, a critical migratory stopover point for birds traveling along the Atlantic Flyway. Nathan Mott Park was the island's first protected open space and is owned by the Block Island Conservancy and managed by the Conservancy. Its trail transverses coastal shrub habitat and globally imperiled morainal grassland, and enters into an area where exotic Japanese black pine trees are dying from disease. Colorful warblers can be found feeding on the insects in the rotting trees. The park's highest hills offer hikers stunning views of the island and surrounding ocean.

CLAY HEAD
200 acres
(401) 466-2129

Block Island's Clay Head trail traverses some of the most spectacular scenery on the eastern seaboard and is considered one of the best places to observe migrating songbirds in the Northeast. Of particular importance are the varieties of fruit-bearing shrubs that provide much-needed food and shelter for these birds in the fall. During the spring, the Conservancy sponsors bird walks to explore places where these songbirds are.

SOUTH CAROLINA

SANDY ISLAND PRESERVE
9,164 acres
(803) 254-9049

Sandy Island, located between the Waccamaw and Great Pee Dee Rivers, is a complex of wetland and upland communities. Mature longleaf pine forests support the endangered red-cockaded woodpecker. Freshwater swamps support an abundance of wildlife, including a large wading bird rookery. The preserve, owned by the South Carolina Department of Transportation and managed by the Conservancy, is open to the public. The island is accessible only by boat.

TEXAS

CLIVE RUNNELLS FAMILY MAD ISLAND MARSH PRESERVE
7,048 acres
(210) 224-8774

The wetlands and coastal prairies of Mad Island Marsh Preserve host more than 250 species of birds each year. Sandhill cranes, alligators, bobcats, armadillos, rattlesnakes, white-tailed deer, and coyotes also make this preserve their home. The preserve is available year-round by appointment only. Call for more details.

GALVESTON BAY PRAIRIE PRESERVE
2,263 acres
(210) 224-8774

Galveston Bay Prairie Preserve, featuring rare coastal prairie habitat, is one of the last three remaining places that support wild Attwater's prairie chickens. In addition to habitat for the prairie chicken, the preserve also provides a home for wintering and migrating grassland songbirds. The site contains excellent wetlands that house black-necked stilts, roseate spoonbills, and many other shorebirds and wading birds. Public access to the preserve is limited. Please call for more information.

UTAH

SCOTT M. MATHESON WETLANDS PRESERVE
900 acres
(435) 259-4629

The Scott M. Matheson Wetlands Preserve, the largest remaining intact wetland along the Colorado River in Utah, is open to the public daily from dawn until dusk. Facilities include a handicapped-accessible one-mile trail loop, a bird blind, and an outdoor classroom site. An additional primitive trail leads to the banks of the Colorado River. Visitors are invited to attend naturalist-guided walks on Saturday morning from March through October. Bird-watching is best in March through May and September through November.

VIRGINIA

VOORHEES NATURE PRESERVE
729 acres
(804) 295-6106

Voorhees Nature Preserve consists of mature coastal plain hardwood forest and a freshwater tidal marsh on the northeast bank of Rappahannock River. Wildlife includes one active bald eagle nest and migratory bird habitat. The preserve features four miles of wooded trails for self-guided walks. Trail maps and brochures are available at the adjacent Westmoreland Berry Farm store. Picnic sites, rest rooms,

and pick-your-own fruits and vegetables are available at Berry Farm. Open weekends, April 22 through December 17.

WASHINGTON

SKAGIT RIVER BALD EAGLE NATURAL AREA
6,000 acres
(206) 343-4344

The Skagit River Bald Eagle Natural Area hosts an impressive winter gathering of bald eagles—one of the four largest in the lower forty-eight states. The gathering each winter coincides with the spawning runs of chum and coho salmon. The Conservancy, the state Department of Fish and Wildlife, and several other agencies own the land. The Conservancy offers stewardship activities from December through February. They include weekly censuses of the eagles, slide presentations, and special guided tours for groups. Two roadside viewing areas are available. Call for more information.

WEST VIRGINIA

CRANESVILLE SWAMP PRESERVE
1,000 acres
(304) 345-4350

This Conservancy preserve features an extensive bog swampland that is open to the public year-round for bird-watching and nature walks. A boardwalk allows visitors to experience the swamp and see sundew, larch trees, and cranberries. Four trails, complete with interpretive signs, guide visitors through unique areas.

WISCONSIN

THOMAS MEMORIAL PRAIRIE
175 acres
(608) 251-8140

Thomas Memorial Prairie, located within the Blue Mounds Prairie Heritage Area, supports more than sixty-eight plant species and thirty-four bird species. Red-winged blackbirds, dickcissels, and eastern meadowlarks are common; upland sandpipers, loggerhead shrikes, and Bell's vireos have also been seen. Butterflies include monarchs, tiger swallowtails, and various species of skippers and sulphurs. The preserve is open to the public year-round except during inclement weather in winter months.

BARNEVELD PRAIRIE PRESERVE
85 acres
(608) 251-8140

Barneveld Prairie, located within the Blue Mounds Prairie Heritage Area, is a matrix of prairie remnants surrounded by agricultural fields, hay fields, and pasture. Its nearly treeless landscape provides habitat for many grassland birds. The preserve harbors rich stands of prairie dropseed, shooting stars, and violets, as well as several rare plants including prairie bush and Indian plantain. The preserve is open to the public.

WYOMING

TENSLEEP PRESERVE
8,500 acres
(307) 332-2971

Tensleep Preserve is located at the junction of the Great Plains, the Rocky Mountains, and the Great Basin. It is nestled in the foothills of the Bighorn Mountains, which are bisected by two deep canyons that are home to seven indigenous plant communities and a variety of wildlife species. Tensleep offers educational and recreational workshops of all sorts, designed to enhance visitors' understanding of the area's rich biological and cultural history. Call for details.